VGM Opportunities Series

OPPORTUNITIES IN
PLASTICS CAREERS

Jan Bone

Foreword by
Larry L. Thomas
President
The Society of the Plastics Industry, Inc.

VGM Career Horizons
a division of *NTC Publishing Group*
Lincolnwood, Illinois USA

Cover Photo Credits

Front cover: upper left, Southern Technical Institute; upper right, Immunex Corporation; lower left, NTC photo; lower right, Dow Chemical Company.

Back cover: upper left, Packaging Corporation of America; upper right, photo of Max Klein, Matcom, Inc., by Roger S. Hart for The Society of the Plastics Industry, Inc.; lower left, *Packaging Magazine;* lower right, RGP Orthotic & Prosthetic Center.

Library of Congress Cataloging-in-Publication Data

Bone, Jan.
    Opportunities in plastics careers / Jan Bone.
       p.   cm. — (VGM opportunities series)

    ISBN 0-8442-8673-7. — ISBN 0-8442-8674-5
    1. Plastics industry and trade—Vocational guidance. I. Title.
II. Series.
HD9661.A2B66   1991
668.4'023'73—dc20   90-50732
                                                                                    CIP

Published by VGM Career Horizons, a division of NTC Publishing Group.
© 1991 by NTC Publishing Group, 4255 West Touhy Avenue,
Lincolnwood (Chicago), Illinois 60646-1975 U.S.A.
All rights reserved. No part of this book may be reproduced, stored
in a retrieval system, or transmitted in any form or by any means,
electronic, mechanical, photocopying, recording or otherwise, without
the prior permission of NTC Publishing Group.
Manufactured in the United States of America.

1 2 3 4 5 6 7 8 9 VP 9 8 7 6 5 4 3 2 1

ABOUT THE AUTHOR

As a little girl growing up during the Depression, Jan Bone played with a celluloid doll and made calls from a Bakelite telephone. Those two plastics were the forerunners of literally hundreds of today's products, created out of petrochemicals. And Jan, who has been a published writer since 1947, says that if she were a young person today, she would pursue a manufacturing career because of its many opportunities for creativity. Jan is an associate member of the Society of Manufacturing Engineers and a member of the Society of the Plastics Industry, Inc. (SPI).

A graduate of Cornell University with an M.B.A. in marketing from Roosevelt University, Jan is a prolific free-lance writer. She is senior writer for the *Chicago Tribune*'s special advertising sections and lead writer for Rand McNally's "Bank Notes," a newsletter for financial publications; she also writes for the Illinois Credit Union League, the National Safety Council, and the Golden Corridor Economic Development Council. Her work has appeared in magazines as diverse as *Family Circle, Woman's World, Bank Administration, Plant Services,* and *Food Engineering.*

Jan has coauthored, with Ron Johnson, *Understanding the Film: A Beginner's Guide to Film Appreciation,* currently in its fourth edition. In the VGM series, she has written *Opportunities in Film*

Careers, Opportunities in Cable Television, Opportunities in Telecommunications Careers, Opportunities in Computer-Aided Design and Computer-Aided Manufacturing (CAD/CAM), Opportunities in Robotics Careers, and *Opportunities in Laser Technology Careers.*

Between 1977 and 1985, Jan was an elected member of the board of trustees of William Rainey Harper Community College in Palatine, Illinois, and served as board secretary from 1979–85.

Jan is listed in *Who's Who of American Women* and *Who's Who in the World.* She has won local, state, and national writing awards.

She is married, mother of four married sons, and the grandmother of Emily and Jennifer.

ACKNOWLEDGMENTS

The author acknowledges with thanks the help given by the following persons and organizations: W. Jerome Baginski, Laurie Barnum, Dave Beechuk, Bob Bone, Janet Borkowski, Lisa Chan, Roger Corneliussen, Mary Beth Curtiss, Beth Davies, K. R. Davis, Jose Fernandes, Norm Gomm, Bob Hamp, James Idol, Janet Krikorian, Dick Koch, Patrick Layhee, Leah Lethbridge, John Meeson, Monroe Miller, Mary Mullane, Tom Nosker, Manny Panos, Michael Parker, Wayne Pearson, Ray Ramsay, Nick R. Schott, Helen Sherwood, Gerald L. Steele, Gregg M. Steinberg, A. Brent Strong, Henry Tschappat, Shelly Weide.

Also Alpha Plastics; Ball State University; Berger, Goldstein Capital Group, Inc.; Brigham Young University; British Consulate/Trade and Investment; British Plastics Federation; Center for Plastics Recycling Research; Chevron Corporation; CIBA-GEIGY Corporation; Department of Industry, Technology and Commerce/New Materials Technology Section (Australia); Dow Plastics; Drexel University; Embassy of Australia; Environment and Plastics Institute of Canada; Ferris State University; Hoechst Celanese; M. David Lowe Personnel Services; Olin Corporation; Plastics Division of Phillips 66 Company; Phillips Petroleum Company; Plastics Institute of America; Plastics Recycling Foundation; Plastics and

Rubber Institute; Ryman, Bell, Green and Michaels, Inc.; Society of Manufacturing Engineers; Society of Plastics Engineers; Society of the Plastics Industry; Society of the Plastics Industry of Canada; Tooling & Manufacturing Association; University of Lowell; Westinghouse.

FOREWORD

During the past 50 years, plastics have developed an amazing presence in our lives, because their range of properties and design technologies make possible otherwise impossible products. In fact, plastics' qualities are so diverse that their benefits tend to be taken for granted: shatter-resistant, water-proof, flexible or rigid, durable or disposable, economical, insulating, non-conducive—and the list goes on.

Indeed, life without plastics would be much less comfortable and much more expensive, while many conveniences now taken for granted would disappear. In short, we live longer, safer, and healthier lives because of plastics.

Plastics also are big business. Plastics represent one of the nation's largest manufacturing industries, providing employment for more than 1.5 million Americans and contributing more than $100 billion annually in sales to our economy. Demand for existing plastics products is expected to increase, and new applications, especially in the area of new alloys and composites, should add to the growth of the industry.

Job prospects for students interested in the plastics industry are excellent. Career possibilities range from manufacturing to research and development to plastics recycling. The plastics industry offers significant challenges for chemists, engineers, machinists, moldmakers, technicians, and business executives.

This book will help you explore the possibilities offered by this dynamic industry. Begin now and get the education and experience that will start you on your way to an exciting career in plastics.

> Larry L. Thomas
> President
> The Society of the Plastics Industry, Inc.

CONTENTS

About the Author iii

Acknowledgments v

Foreword vii

1. **Plastics: An Important Industry** 1
   Plastics are everywhere. Composites. History of plastics. Plastics and additives. Plastics on a global scale. Groups of plastics. Advantages of plastics.

2. **Who Works in Plastics?** 13
   The S.I.C. codes. The SPI labor survey. BLS figures. BLS projections. How trends affect your chances.

3. **Planning Your Education** 21
   Researching schools. Choosing your courses. Engineering. Specific programs. Seminars.

4. **Financing Your Education** 40
   Start early. TMA apprenticeships. Scholarships. Co-operative programs. Summer work.

x   *Opportunities in Plastics Careers*

5. **Personal Qualities** 49
   Teamwork. Autonomy. Enthusiasm. Responsible behavior. Commitment to learning. Technical savvy—and a lot more.

6. **Finding a Job** 53
   Start early. Do your homework. Trade journals. Using a personnel service.

7. **Keeping Up: Seminars, Workshops, Conventions** . . 65
   Seminars and workshops. Conventions.

8. **Plastics Research and Development** 68
   What annual reports show. R&D at Dow Plastics. How Dow Plastics recruits. Dow locations.

9. **Technical Sales and Marketing** 75
   Hiring the veterans. The hiring process. Phillips' plastics portfolio. The recruiting process. Technical sales and marketing training. Future opportunities.

10. **Making Engineering Plastics** 86
    About the plant. Operators and operator-helpers. Other plant employees. Recruitment and hiring.

11. **Opportunities in a Plant that Uses Plastics** 92
    Customized operations. On the factory floor. Workers' qualifications. Future opportunities.

12. **Opportunities in Plastics Recycling** 98
    Environmental issues. Myths about plastics. Plastics Recycling Foundation. What it takes to recycle. Plastics recycling jobs. Recycling organizations.

13. **Women and Minorities** 115

   Concentrate on science and math. Society of Women Engineers. Financial aid for women and minorities. Minority recruitment. Special help. Southeastern Consortium for Minorities. National Society of Black Engineers. Other organizations. On the job.

14. **International Opportunities** 131

   Plastics in Canada. Opportunities in Great Britain. Opportunities in Australia.

Appendix A: Periodicals 143

CHAPTER 1

PLASTICS: AN IMPORTANT INDUSTRY

In Mike Nichols's classic 1968 film *The Graduate*, Dustin Hoffman, who plays Benjamin Braddock, is cornered at his 21st birthday party by his parents' friends, who want to know what he's going to do with his future.

"I want to talk to you," says one balding neighbor, leading Benjamin aside. "I want to say one word to you—just one word. Are you listening?"

"Yes, sir. I am."

"PLASTICS."

Hoffman is silent.

"There's a great future in plastics, Benjamin. Think about it."

PLASTICS ARE EVERYWHERE

Then, as now, viewers roared at the incident. But actually, the man gave young Benjamin good advice. Today the plastics industry is a multibillion-dollar business—a business whose products touch virtually all facets of our lives; a business growing globally, says Dow Chemical Company, at an estimated 4.5 percent annually.

You may be wearing clothing made from plastics* fibers: nylon, Orlon, and acrylics are a few of the familiar names. Your shoes may have plastics uppers or soles. You may be carrying a wallet or a purse made from plastics.

Many of your daily activities involve plastics products. You may drink your morning coffee from a foam cup, microwave a Danish pastry wrapped in plastic wrap, and pour your milk from a gallon container made from plastics. You may carry groceries into your home in a plastics bag, and you probably put your trash out in plastics containers.

Many cars have plastics parts: front fenders on Cadillac's DeVille and Fleetwood models, bumper beams and fascia on Hyundai's Sonatas, radiator housing in the GM Corvette, and composite bumper beams on the Honda Accord are examples. In fact, General Motors has announced that during the nineties, it plans to produce one million plastic-body cars a year, or about one-fifth of its current United States production. Using plastics in cars reduces weight—helping cars to be more fuel-efficient. Using plastics parts allows the manufacturer to save money on labor costs, too, because the color can be molded in, and the part doesn't have to be painted.

Plastics offer other advantages to vehicle manufacturers. Monsanto's Saflex plastic interlayer makes automobile glass shatter-resistant. Two other plastics from Monsanto (Lustran Elite HH, a high heat plastic, and Lustran Elite LGA, a low-gloss plastic for interior trim) have been created for the automotive industry to satisfy specific customer needs.

---

*The industry uses the term "plastics" to refer to plastics products and plastics materials. Such usage avoids confusion with the term "plastic," which describes any material, such as clay, that can be pressed into various shapes.

Plastics products meet many consumer needs. The computer keyboard on which this manuscript was written is made from plastics. Your telephone has plastics parts. And don't forget Tupperware, the plastic food storage containers that have been around for over forty years. Ninety-four percent of American homes contain a Tupperware product. In 1989, 88 million people, mostly women, went to Tupperware parties around the world. About one out of four were Americans. On the average, somewhere in the world, a Tupperware party begins every 2.7 seconds. In the United States, on the average, a Tupperware party begins every 10 seconds. More than 50,000 Americans a day attend Tupperware parties, and there are 60,000 parties a week.

The list of plastics products is seemingly endless: plastic bags and containers; polyvinylchloride pipe, siding, and containers; polyester fibers and resins for clothing, tires, seatbelts, and protective coatings. High density polyethylene is used to make plastic bottles, jugs, pails, and plastic pipe for sewage and drainage systems. Low density polyethylene is used to manufacture bread bags, shrink packaging, disposable diapers, coatings for milk cartons, and overlids for cans. Plastics products are everywhere.

Where Plastics Are Used

When the 25 largest U.S. manufacturing industries are compared, miscellaneous plastics products rank fifth, according to Department of Commerce figures, with 1989 industry shipments of nearly $56 billion. Manufacturing of plastics materials and resins, a category the government tracks separately, ranks 15th in the top 25, with 1989 shipments of nearly $26 billion.

In many of today's major markets, plastics and plastic products play a significant role. They're used in transportation and in packaging. In building and construction, plastics play a major role: pipe, conduit, and fittings; siding, flooring, insulation, panels, doors, windows, skylights, bathroom units, gratings, and railings. Plastics are components of home and industrial appliances, communications equipment, resistors, and batteries. They're used in furniture, carpeting, blinds, and wall coverings. Plastics are important—and controversial—in disposable goods, including picnic ware and disposable cups. In fact, a new, and increasingly significant, technology has begun to emerge in plastics recycling. From health care products and lab supplies to hobby equipment and luggage; from industrial machinery to inks, adhesives, and coatings; plastics have become an essential ingredient of nearly everything you touch and use. For instance, when you ride a bike, you may be using products made with plastics fibers—Kevlar in your helmet and tires, Lycra and Coolmax in your cycling outfit, and even a new aerodynamic wheel, designed and manufactured with advanced composites technology.

COMPOSITES

Consider composites made from plastics, and the list of products and job opportunities multiplies. Technically speaking, *composites* are made of two different kinds of material chosen because of the synergy, or added value, from putting them together. The properties and qualities of each are enhanced when they're joined. Composites may—but don't have to—involve plastics. Dr. A. Brent Strong, industry consultant and an associate professor at Brigham Young University, defines composites as "the combination of a reinforcement material, such as a particle or fiber, in a matrix or binder material." Under his admittedly narrow definition, polymers are included as matrix material, with fibers and polymers included as options for reinforcements. The matrix can be thought of as the glue that binds the reinforcements together and protects the reinforcement from the effects of environment.

Composites are used in a number of industries. In airplanes, for example, interior sidewalls, partitions, and floor panels are often made of composites. The Voyager aircraft, which flew nonstop around the world without refueling, is nearly 100 percent composite; it could accomplish this feat because the body of the aircraft was used as a fuel tank, due to the excellent solvent resistance of the composite materials.

Body panels of cars and vans are often made of composites; so are truck tractor bodies, sleeper units, and often entire trailer bodies. Pleasure boats and racing boats have hulls, masts, and other structures made of fiberglass and polyester—a composite. Printed circuit boards use composites as a substrate. Building panels for office partitions, corrugated fiberglass and polyester panels for carports and patio covers, and even interior panels on BART, the San Francisco Bay Area Rapid Transit System, are made of composites.

Recreational equipment is often made of composites. Shafts and heads of golf clubs, tennis racquets, archery bows and arrows, skis and ski poles, water skis, bobsleds, bicycles, and race cars use composites because of their stiffness, strength, and light weight. In fact, the first modern application of composites was a glass-reinforced phenolic-nylon fishing pole created in 1945.

HISTORY OF PLASTICS

The number of uses for plastics and composites is growing daily as new products and processes are developed by scientists and engineers. It wasn't always so, of course. *Plastic* (easily molded) materials have been around since prehistoric times; even clay on a riverbank can be described as plastic. But *plastics,* as we use the term today, date back to before the Civil War and are closely tied in with the rubber industry. "Hard rubber," discovered in

1851, was the first chemically modified natural material. Materials such as Parkesine (developed by English inventor Alexander Parkes in 1862) and Xylonite (developed in the 1870s by an English associate of Parkes) had been introduced, but they were unsuccessful commercially.

Celluloid

Shortly after the Civil War, John Wesley Hyatt, an American printer, also began experimenting with cellulose nitrate, the material Parkes had used as a basis for Parkesine. Manufacturers of billiard balls, then made of ivory, found the demand for elephant tusks exceeded the supply. One New York manufacturer offered a $10,000 prize for a satisfactory substitute. While Hyatt didn't win the prize, he developed celluloid—the first commercially viable plastic.

Celluloid was clear and solid but could be tinted virtually any color. In the twenty years after Hyatt's 1872 patent, over 2,500 different articles were being produced from it. Because celluloid could be colored, dentists used it to make the gums in sets of false teeth. Celluloid also was used to make white collars, cuffs, and false shirt fronts; men wore them in preference to linen and cotton because the plastic could be washed clean with soap and water. Celluloid dolls and toys, celluloid flexible windows that snapped on the side curtains of cars before closed sedans were built, celluloid toothbrushes, frames for eyeglasses, piano keys, and combs were just a few of the many articles created from Hyatt's synthetic material. Celluloid had two significant drawbacks, however; it was highly flammable, and it couldn't be molded.

Bakelite

Just before the turn of the century, German chemists found they could take casein, produced by adding a compound to milk, and modify it to make knitting needles, buttons, beads, and adhesives. Then Dr. Leo Baekeland, a Belgian chemist who had moved to Yonkers, New York, began to experiment with phenol (carbolic acid) and formaldehyde. Eventually he developed Bakelite, a dark plastic resin that could be molded. Later, a New Jersey inventor mixed wood flour and asbestos with the plastic, for added strength. Useful products could be made from the new Bakelite. When the telephone companies decided to make their handsets from Bakelite, the plastic became a commercial success.

Between 1909, when Bakelite was introduced, and 1927, there were virtually no new artificial plastics. The following years, however, brought many new discoveries as chemists worldwide began to synthesize various compounds. Urea-based resins were an important breakthrough because, unlike Bakelite and other phenol compounds, these resins could be used to mold light-colored articles. Another important discovery was cellulose acetate, a compound very like cellulose nitrate in structure, but much safer.

By World War II, today's major plastics were being developed: polyvinyl chloride, low density polyethylene, polystyrene, and polymethyl methacrylate. Because the war disrupted the supply of many natural materials, including natural rubber, chemists began researching polymer chemistry intensively. Eventually, more plastics materials were developed and produced commercially.

PLASTICS AND ADDITIVES

Today, plastics materials are broadly classified into two major groups: thermoset plastics and thermoplastics. *Thermoset plastics* are set by heat; that is, once they've been heated and molded to shape, they keep that shape permanently. *Thermoplastics* can also be heated and molded. They, too, keep their shape once they've been cooled. However, thermoplastic substances can be reheated and molded to a different shape.

Synthetic plastics are polymers—large molecules formed from many smaller molecules that are joined together in extremely long chains. The chains contain carbon atoms, as well as atoms of other elements. Sometimes plastics chemists use heat to string the chains together. In another technique in which water is given off as a waste product, they combine chemical substances. In still another method, chemists reform the polymers that exist in natural materials.

Most polymers, however, have little practical value without a small percentage of chemical additives that give the materials useful properties. Additives help improve processing and allow polymers to be used for specific applications. Over 4,000 individual additives exist. They're classified into four major types:

1. Reaction controls (catalysts, initiators, auxiliary processing materials)
2. Processing additives (blowing agents and lubricants)
3. Stabilizers (antioxidants, heat stabilizers, light or ultraviolet stabilizers, preservatives)
4. Performance additives (fillers and reinforcements, plasticizers—added to give flexibility, colorants, impact modifiers, flame retardants, anti-static agents, coupling agents).

Most additives are inert fillers. Many additives are used in manufacturing processes, and they do not wind up as part of the finished polymers. Plasticizers, however, can account for 40 percent of some plastics products, including insulating material for wire and cable and artificial leather made from polyvinyl chloride (PVC).

PLASTICS ON A GLOBAL SCALE

With worldwide use of plastics and plastics products on an upswing, your future career in plastics may take you outside the United States. Du Pont–certified Stainmaster residential carpet is sold in more than 50 nations. The company's licensing agreement to produce industrial nylon in Indonesia follows a joint venture under way in Turkey, with another joint venture awaiting government approval in India. Du Pont is opening a new plant for Nomex aramid fiber in Spain, and Kevlar aramid fiber in Japan—supplementing existing plants for Nomex in Japan, Kevlar in Northern Ireland, and Tyvek spunbonded olefin in Luxembourg. The world's largest producer of nylon intermediates such as adipic acid, Du Pont also is building an adipic acid plant in Singapore.

Dow also does a great deal of business outside the United States. Dow added more than 180 million pounds of new polystyrene capacity to its Hong Kong plant in 1990 to meet increasing demand in the Pacific Basin. In West Germany, a compounding plant for Calibre polycarbonate (a new engineering thermoplastic) came on line in 1990; a second, in 1991. Dow's joint venture with Sumitomo Chemical Company, Ltd. for engineering thermoplastics resulted in a new polycarbonate railroad train in Japan. In Taiwan and Colombia, trains have been manufactured from polyol, a type of plastic. A joint venture in Hungary to manufacture Styrofoam insulation benefited from changing conditions in Eastern Europe, and Dow's propylene oxide plants in Canada and Brazil have been expanded.

BASF, a major international chemical company headquartered in Germany, has plants in Korea, Canada, Belgium, Spain, and the United States.

ARCO Chemical Company is involved in a joint venture in Indonesia, the first polyols plant in the country. They target production for domestic use and for export to growing markets throughout the Pacific Rim countries. ARCO also is increasing polyols production at its joint-venture plants in South Korea and Japan and at a new plant in France. The company has plants in France, the Netherlands, Taiwan, and Korea which produce propylene glycol—a food additive "generally recognized as safe" by the U.S. Food and Drug Administration. Propylene glycol, a preferred ingredient in solvents when toxicity is an issue, and an "environmentally friendly" product, is also a major ingredient in a new aircraft anti-icer.

GROUPS OF PLASTICS

Because many jobs in plastics technology require familiarity with the characteristics of plastics and additives, the man or woman who plans a career in plastics technology will find it helpful to know and understand chemistry and chemical processes.

Five resins account for about two-thirds of all plastics sales: low-density polyethylene, high-density polyethylene, polyvinyl chloride, polypropylene, and polystyrene. Other *commodity thermoplastics* include polyethylene terephtalate (PET), being used more and more in packaging, and nylon. These plastics are produced in high volumes, at relatively low cost. Because they soften when heated and can be remolded, they may be candidates for recycling.

Engineering thermoplastics, used in the construction, electric, electronic, and transportation industries, are produced in low volume, at a high cost.

Thermosets, which make up about 20 percent of the U.S. plastics market, are low-volume materials, compared to thermoplastics. Major markets for them include the industries of building and construction, transportation, and furniture and furnishings. Polyurethane and phenolic, both resins, are sold in sizable quantities, predominantly for products like building insulation.

Multicomponent plastics and laminations combine various plastics or use plastics together with other materials, such as paper or metal foil. Most multicomponent plastics are used for packaging because they combine properties of different materials. For example, plastic ketchup bottles are made from several plastics: an exterior plastic for appearance and strength, an adhesive which holds different plastics together and attaches the label, a special oxygen-barrier plastic, and an interior plastic that withstands exposure to fats and acids.

ADVANTAGES OF PLASTICS

Plastics are replacing other materials because plastics often save weight, cost, and processing time. They resist corrosion and environmental effects because they're inert. Plastics can be tailored to suit special needs. They can be made rigid, flexible, or stretchable. They can "breathe" or be impermeable.

Although plastics are often more expensive to produce than alternative materials like glass, aluminum, steel, and paper, the properties of plastics may give them a cost-effective advantage. Thus, plastics often represent a better value for manufacturers with specific needs.

Plastics are versatile. Depending on the type of plastic material, you can mold, extrude, bend, twist, turn, paint, coat, cut, melt, heat, cool, reinforce, decorate, or join it for literally hundreds of applications.

Given the variety of plastics and their advantages, the future looks bright for those who want careers in plastics technology. All these industrial and consumer plastics products mean jobs—for those who design them, produce them, and sell them. One of those jobs may be yours.

Thousands of companies process plastics into finished products, while only a few hundred manufacture plastic resins. Consequently, if you want a career in plastics technology, you may well have a greater chance of joining a "user" company, rather than a primary producer.

No one book has all the answers to your questions on plastics. But *Opportunities in Plastics Careers* will give you information about some of plastics' components, and lead you to sources for more detailed information in specific areas.

The plastics industry has its own special character, value, and opportunities for those who work in the industry. Perhaps it will be special for you too.

CHAPTER 2

WHO WORKS IN PLASTICS?

How many people work in plastics technology careers? What do they do? How can you find out? There are no hard-and-fast, absolute numbers available. But data from various sources will give you some idea of the scope of the industry and the outlook for future employment.

THE S.I.C. CODES

The Standard Industrial Classification System (S.I.C.), developed by the U.S. Bureau of the Census, classifies all manufacturing into 20 major industry groups. Each has a two-digit code. Thus, #25 is furniture and fixtures, and #35 is machinery, except electrical. Each major industry group is further subdivided into about 150 industry subgroups which are designated by a three-digit code. For example, #282 is "Plastics materials and synthetic resins, synthetic rubber, cellulosic and other manmade fibers, except glass," and #289 is "miscellaneous chemical products." Each industry is further subdivided into approximately 450 product categories designated by a four-digit code. Category #2821 is "Plastics Materials, Synthetic Resins, and Nonvulcanizable Elastomers'' and #2891 is "Adhesives and Sealants"—which includes plastics adhesives.

The codes are specific and describe industries, by product. For instance, products of industry code #2821 include cellulose plastics materials, casein plastics, and these resins: phenolic and other tar acid, urea and melamine, vinyl, styrene, alkyd, acrylic, polyethylene, polypropylene, rosin-modified, petroleum polymer, and miscellaneous resins (including polyamide resins, silicones, polyisobutylenes, polyesters, polycarbonate resins, acetal resins, and fluorohydrocarbon resins).

You can learn more about S.I.C. codes from the *Standard Industrial Classification Manual,* a reference book available at most school or public libraries. Or you can buy an inexpensive listing of all S.I.C. codes relating to the plastics industry. Order *The Plastics Industry S.I.C. Codes* from The Society of the Plastics Industry (SPI), Attention: Literature Sales, Suite 400, 1275 K Street, NW, Washington, D.C. 20005.

Knowing the S.I.C. codes helps you to locate and understand data about industry statistics. For instance, for each four-digit S.I.C. number, the Census of Manufacturers provides the number of establishments—subclassified by location, number of employees, annual sales, and net worth.

THE SPI LABOR SURVEY

Quantitative information on jobs in plastics processing companies is compiled annually by the Financial Management Committee of The Society of the Plastics Industry, Inc. (SPI). Executives from over 70 plastics-processing firms throughout the United States are members of this committee; each representative has a background in finance, management, and manufacturing. The group meets regularly during the year to monitor its various survey programs and discuss industry problems. Besides the labor survey, the committee also sponsors a financial and operating ratios survey, a salary and sales policy survey, and an employee benefits survey. All can be purchased from the Literature Sales Department, The Society of the Plastics Industry, Inc., 1275 K Street, NW, Suite 400, Washington, D.C. 20005.

The labor survey reports data from over 200 SPI member companies representing over 250 plants. It provides an industry basis for companies to compare their compensation practices to all companies, as well as to firms in the same geographic region.

An especially useful feature of the labor survey is its "Job Descriptions for Plastics Manufacturing Plants." This section of the survey gives examples of typical work requirements in plants engaged in blow molding, compression molding, injection molding, extrusion, and reinforced plastics. These composite job descriptions are based on individual classifications received from many manufacturing plants. For instance, here is the job description for a setup person and/or troubleshooter in molding and extrusion work:

> Sets up molds in presses so that presses are ready for production when setup is completed. Removes mold and auxiliary equipment from press, sets next mold, locates and fastens on press, sets ejection, sets and adjusts to prescribed stroke, changing piping as required. Sets and adjusts machine controls. Sets up and prepares auxiliary equipment such as insert loads, material loaders, shrink frames, preheaters, finishing tools and checks operation of press. Operates under detailed instructions and specifications, but requires considerable ingenuity to improvise and adapt when necessary. May instruct trainees who assist. . . in mold and equipment changes and setups.
>
> Works closely with shift foreman and is capable of assuming temporary supervisory responsibilities in the absence of the foreman. Diagnoses and corrects problem in setup and

operation of molds, presses, and other equipment. Sets and periodically adjusts machines' operating conditions. May perform routine maintenance, give breaks, fill hoppers, or set molds as required.

According to the 1989 SPI Labor Survey, the weighted average hourly rate for this position (accounting for geographical differences) was $8.97. Salaries ranged from $7.83 in the Southeast to $9.66 in New England.

In 1989, a working foreman in a molding job earned a national weighted average hourly rate of $10.20 for compression molding—slightly less in injection molding ($9.47) and in blow molding ($9.42).

Slightly more than half of salaried first-line supervisors received Christmas or other bonuses, generally based on such factors as percent of earnings, length of service, company or plant profits, or employee performance and merit. SPI's 1989 Labor Survey showed that first-line supervisors in compression molding had a national, weighted, average monthly base salary of $2,099; those in injection molding, $2,236; and those in blow molding, $2,683. About two-thirds of the plants included in the 1989 survey paid overtime to shift supervisors; the majority of those doing so paid overtime when supervisors worked over 40 hours a week.

BLS FIGURES

The Bureau of Labor Statistics also tracks workers in various industries. Their statistics show that in 1986 companies in the S.I.C. category for "rubber and miscellaneous plastics products" employed 793,410 workers. Sixty-four percent of these people worked in factories molding primary plastics or fabricating mis-

cellaneous finished plastics products. Within the industry, these five occupations had the most workers:
1. Plastic molding and casting machine operators and tenders
2. Assemblers and fabricators, except machine, electrical, electronic, and precision
3. Hand packers and packagers
4. First-line supervisors of production
5. Production inspectors, testers, graders, sorters, samplers, and weighers

BLS PROJECTIONS

Newer reports from the Bureau of Labor Statistics (BLS) give us more clues about job prospects. First of all, there will be fewer people coming into the U.S. labor force. During the years 1976–1988, the labor force grew at 2 percent annually; in the years between 1988 and 2000, under moderate projections, annual growth will be 1.2 percent. By 2000, the labor force is projected to total 141 million people.

The role of women in the work force is increasing; in 1976, they made up 40 percent, and by 2000, BLS projects them at 47 percent. Young people age 16–24 were 24 percent of the labor force in 1976; by 2000, they are expected to be only 16 percent. BLS expects more African Americans, Hispanics, and Asians in the labor force—primarily because of population growth, but, in the case of Hispanics, also because of increased participation.

Of the 18 million total new jobs expected by 2000, services will dominate. About half of the new jobs will be in retail trade, health services, and business services. Manufacturing is expected to decrease by 314,000 jobs by the year 2000. However, significant gains are expected for professional specialty occupations within the field, especially in engineering and technical and related

18   Opportunities in Plastics Careers

support occupations. Jobs for operators, fabricators, and laborers are expected to decline—both in absolute terms, and as a proportion of total manufacturing employment. Technological innovations and improved production processes, such as robotics or flexible manufacturing systems, are partly responsible.

BLS projections within manufacturing show 715,000 engineers employed in 1988; 833,000 are expected to be employed by the year 2000. In 1988, 495,000 engineering and science technicians and technologists were working in manufacturing; by 2000, 552,000 are expected to be so employed.

Some jobs are declining, according to BLS's *Outlook 2000,* a report from the U.S. Department of Labor. Jobs for machine forming operators and tenders who work in metal and plastic (BLS doesn't separate the two) are expected to decline by 18.4 percent in all industries. Jobs for machine tool-cutting operators and tenders, metal and plastic, will decline by 14.9 percent; and jobs for all other metal and plastic machine setters, operators, and related workers will decline by 11.5 percent, using BLS's "moderate" projections. Taken into account in those predictions: BLS's specific assumptions for plastics materials and synthetics, which say there will be "some outgrowth as plastics continue to substitute for metals, for example, carbon fiber resin in autos and airplanes. However, growth will be somewhat dampened by slowdown in synthetic fibers as apparel production slows." Increasing automation will influence job losses as plants begin to use more computer-controlled equipment.

HOW TRENDS AFFECT YOUR CHANCES

What does this information mean to your chances for a career in plastics technology? It's good to remember that all the data in the world and the best projections won't give you definite answers on which to base your career decision. Projections, after all, are based on assumptions that may or may not be accurate. Industries always have room for good people who like what they are doing, enjoy the field, want to move ahead, and are willing to work hard. However, the information given previously is worth considering for its implications.

If your sights are limited to actually working in a plastics plant on a machine, or even several machines, automated processes and computer-controlled equipment may well cut down your chances for jobs. Even in a small plastics plant, a pick-and-place robot or a computer-controlled turntable can eliminate a person who otherwise would move material into place and handle it.

However, the person with the skills to reprogram the robot or the computer controls that set the machines—in short, the person with technical skills—has a better chance of getting and keeping a job.

The Office of Technology Assessment, an arm of the United States Congress, points out changes in manufacturing technology and human resources requirements. In the past, a recent report says, most manufacturing workers learned their jobs by the sides of more experienced workers, and an ordinary grammar school or high school education was plenty of preparation for a production worker in manufacturing. Today, with automation affecting more workplaces and less automated work being exported overseas, production jobs in manufacturing require more conceptual knowledge—and often competence in statistical process control and management of computerized equipment. In short, more is being demanded of manufacturing workers.

The more you know, the more schooling you have, the more chance you have for increasing your earning power. In 1987, engineering technicians and technologists had median annual earnings of $24,489 (half of them earned more; half, less). BLS says those with less than a high school education had median earnings of $16,207; those with a high school diploma, $21,358; those with one or two years of college, $23,830; and those with at least a four-year college degree, $28,004. Salaries for degreed, qualified engineers are, of course, substantially higher.

Obviously, then, you'll increase your earning power by acquiring skills and training. How can you start?

CHAPTER 3

PLANNING YOUR EDUCATION

To prepare for a career in plastics technology, what and where should you study? How do you locate schools that offer the courses you need? How do you even know what you need to learn?

Because so much of plastics technology deals with properties of various polymers (the long chains of molecules that make up plastics), you should take courses in math and science—especially chemistry—during high school. These courses will make you academically eligible for engineering studies. You may not necessarily major in engineering, but by taking four years of high school math and science, you'll have more options open.

RESEARCHING SCHOOLS

One of the best ways to get information on post–high school study is to check reference books at your school or public library. Start with *Lovejoy's College Guide*, a reference book covering approximately 2,500 American colleges and universities. *Lovejoy's* section on career curricula and special programs lists over 60 schools offering degree programs in plastics/polymers science. Some of them are community colleges that offer an associate degree program; the majority have bachelor's degree programs. You can also check listings under manufacturing engineering or materials science.

You'll want to write directly to the admissions office of any school that interests you; addresses of the colleges and universities are also listed in *Lovejoy's*. Ask each school for a catalog, admissions information, and any flyers or brochures describing programs in plastics technology or related subjects. Often, you'll find "plastics" described under "polymer science" or "polymer engineering." Sometimes plastics is listed under "technology," "materials science," or "materials engineering." You can also ask for information on any certificate programs a particular school might offer.

Another good source of information is *Listing of Institutions Which Offer Graduate or Undergraduate Plastics/Polymer Programs in the United States and Canada*. The publication, issued annually, is available from the Society of Plastics Engineers, 14 Fairfield Drive, Brookfield, Connecticut 06804.

The *Catalog of Polymer Science and Engineering Programs*, which includes descriptions of specific facilities at each educational institution, can be ordered from the Plastics Institute of America, Inc., Suite 100, 277 Fairfield Road, Fairfield, New Jersey 07004-1932.

If your eventual goal is to work in a plastics manufacturing plant or laboratory, or to work in a manufacturing enterprise that uses plastics as a raw material, the more you know about manufacturing engineering and technology, the better off you'll be. You can learn about some of these programs by reading *Directory of Manufacturing Education in Colleges, Universities, and Technical Institutes*. This directory can be purchased from the Society of Manufacturing Engineers, One SME Drive, P.O. Box 930, Dearborn, Michigan 48121. It describes each school, listing names and phone numbers of key people to contact; manufacturing degrees, undergraduate, and graduate-level courses offered; and types of manufacturing laboratories and equipment available at each school. The 250-page book also indicates whether cooperative education programs and night school courses are available.

CHOOSING YOUR COURSES

One reason it's difficult to "lock in" on a course of study is that different colleges and universities emphasize different aspects of the plastics industry. Remember, too, that the vast majority of people in the plastics industry today have not had any formal education in plastics. As Nick R. Schott and Rudolph D. Deanin of the University of Lowell explain, these people have come from related fields such as chemistry, chemical engineering, mechanical engineering, and biology. They have learned about plastics directly through their work experience, at great cost to their employers and to themselves in terms of both time and money. Whenever they change projects, they have to learn each new subject again from the bottom up. During a professional career, each of them becomes a specialist in several narrow areas, but they rarely acquire a broad enough education to work freely and expertly in the field of plastics as a whole.

As the field grows more diverse and more sophisticated, the need for a broad, thorough educational background in plastics becomes more critical, both for employer and employee. Yet there is still no formal training requirement—no mandated single set of courses you can point to and say, "These represent all I need to know about plastics."

Because there is no single "right" course of study that will automatically prepare and qualify you for a career in plastics technology, you may decide to major in chemistry, engineering, manufacturing technology, materials science, or similar subjects as an undergraduate—specializing in polymer science for your graduate work. You may want to look for schools and colleges that allow you to take courses across department lines. You can cut costs by looking specifically for programs that allow you to co-op—alternating semesters as a full-time student with working for a company. You may want to check out a school's policy on internships and the ability of its students to land them. You'll certainly want to ask a program director how many graduates are working in the industry—and how they're doing.

ENGINEERING

The Accreditation Board of Engineering and Technology (ABET) defines *engineering* as "the profession in which a knowledge of the mathematical and natural sciences gained by study, experience, and practice is applied with judgment to develop ways to utilize, economically, the materials and forces of nature for the benefit of [humanity]." Engineering involves a high degree of creative activity in identifying theories and developing them into practical applications.

Engineering technologists are usually required to take fewer math and science courses than engineers take. Instead, more emphasis is placed in laboratory work, skill development, and applied engineering. In general, engineering technologists are graduates of baccalaureate programs. ABET defines *engineering technology* as "that part of the technological field which requires the application of scientific and engineering knowledge and methods combined with technical skills in support of engineering activities. It lies in the occupational spectrum between the [craftperson] and the engineer at the end of the spectrum closest to the engineer."

Some colleges have two-year programs that train graduates as engineering technicians. In geographic regions that have a number of plastics processing plants or firms which make end-user products from plastics raw materials, community colleges often have set up associate degree programs or certificate programs that train students for hands-on or supervisors' jobs in the industry. Often such courses lead to the Associate in Applied Science degree, or to a certificate, but may not be automatically transferable towards a baccalaureate degree. Be sure you know and understand the policies about transfer before you enroll.

SPECIFIC PROGRAMS

Elgin Community College

One example of technical training that helps you qualify for entry-level jobs or enhance your skills is the program offered at a suburban Chicago community college. Elgin Community College, about 45 miles northwest of Chicago, offers a typical certificate program. The Chicago metropolitan area and the Fox Valley, in particular, are a hub for the plastics industry, with over 1,500 firms there making or processing plastics. In the late 1960s, Elgin Community College became one of the first colleges in the United States to offer plastics training programs.

Today, a four-semester program leads to a certificate of "vocational specialist in thermoplastics injection molding." The program emphasizes technical specialty courses in injection and clamp mechanism, thermoplastics materials, molds, and processes of injection. Supplementary courses in basic math, graphics, and communications are part of the course work.

Students are expected to be working in the thermoplastics injection molding industry while they take classes; college officials attempt to help with job placement, if students are not already employed. Graduates of the program are prepared for entry-level employment as mold setters or processing troubleshooters on production injection molding machines. For information, write to Dean of Industrial Technology, Elgin Community College, Elgin, Illinois 60120.

Ivy Tech

Indiana's Technical College, Ivy Tech, offers an Associate in Applied Science degree in plastics technology. Part of the statewide Indiana vocational technical college system, Ivy Tech is located in Evansville, Indiana—nucleus of the "plastics valley," which is home to more than 110 plastics manufacturing companies that employ more than 10,000 persons, according to a study by Batelle. The same study identified an unmet need for training for entry-level operators, technical employees, engineers, and managers. Plastics technology training at Ivy Tech was designed to meet that need.

Students take courses in such subjects as introduction to polymer science, computer fundamentals, computer numerical control (CNC) machining, extrusion processes, injection molding, and thermoplastics production processes. Additional custom training is offered to those currently working in plastics manufacturing—both in extrusion technology and injection molding. For information, write to Ivy Tech, Indiana Vocational Technical College, 3501 First Avenue, Evansville, Indiana 47710.

Ball State University

Under the manufacturing engineering technology program at Ball State, students interested in plastics choose that specialization after taking core courses in math, science, and computers.

Hands-on experience in injection molding, extrusion, blow molding, compression molding, bead foam molding, rotational molding, dip coating, heat sealing, hot foil stamping, and pad printing is part of the introductory course; later courses involve CAD/CAM work in computer mold design. Students also design thermoformed products, build necessary molds, set up small production runs, and run quality control tests on molded and extruded parts and blown films.

Also part of Ball State University is its Plastics Research Center, which conducts studies of microprocessor controls, new plastics technologies, and the effectiveness of CAD/CAM and robotics. The research center, which involves students in research and service projects for the industry, works closely with Indiana plastics manufacturers.

For information, write the Department of Industry and Technology, Ball State University, Muncie, Indiana 47306.

Brigham Young University

The plastics curriculum at Brigham Young University lies chiefly within the Department of Manufacturing Engineering and Technology. Courses concerned with plastics include courses on engineering materials, plastics materials and processes, polymer materials and processes, and introduction to composites. Students have several elective courses which could include chemistry and chemical engineering courses related to the manufacture of plastics, and mechanical engineering courses related to design concepts of plastics and composites.

Brigham Young University offers an interdisciplinary program of graduate study and research in the area of plastics and composite materials involving students and faculty in the Departments of Chemical Engineering, Manufacturing Engineering and Technology, and Mechanical Engineering. The program leads to M.S. and

Ph.D. degrees. Areas of research include composite materials manufacturing and fabrication; fiber and matrix surfaces; fiber, matrix, and laminate properties; and damage and fatigue.

Brigham Young University also offers a master's degree in computer integrated manufacturing, designed specifically for the engineering technology graduate. A student can specialize in plastics in any of these programs. Course work can be tailored to fit the student's interest, and several professors would advise the students to do research work in plastics, composites, or related studies. Course offerings at the graduate level include courses in advanced polymer structure, processing, and related subjects.

For additional information, write: Technology Department, 435 CTB, Brigham Young University, Provo, Utah 84602.

Drexel University

Drexel University's courses in polymers and related technology fall under Materials Engineering. At the undergraduate level, students begin with a fundamentals course that covers molecular solids, molecular chains, polymeric materials, glassy and crystalline polymers, and rubber elasticity. They continue with courses in topics such as materials processing; structure of materials, including heat treatment of polymers; materials degradation; and introduction to bioengineering, which includes selection and performance of implant materials.

Qualified students with undergraduate degrees in physical or biological sciences may enter Drexel University's graduate program in materials engineering. However, non-engineering graduates must take an appropriate number of the undergraduate engineering courses to supplement their background. Graduate courses are offered both on a regular full-time basis and on a part-time basis.

Drexel's graduate program in materials engineering allows students to specialize in polymeric materials. A polymer processing laboratory includes laboratory-scale extruders, injection molding machines, an ultrasonic compaction machine, and a 10,000-psi Dake press. For more information, write to Drexel University, Philadelphia, Pennsylvania 19104.

Ferris State University

Stressing hands-on instruction in manufacturing and processing, the plastics engineering technology program at Ferris State University offers a two-year Associate in Applied Science degree and a four-year Bachelor of Science degree. Both programs require a 10-week industrial internship.

Although most graduates from the bachelor's program go on to work for large companies, a significant percentage of them are starting their own businesses, according to program director Henry Tschppat, who feels the entrepreneurial spirit is flourishing at Ferris. One reason, he feels, is that Ferris requires students to take certain business courses, in addition to significant time they spend working with plastics processing equipment. Ferris State's flexible programs allow students to specialize in areas of the industry that are experiencing labor shortages. Students may earn an associate degree in industrial chemistry through the university's chemistry department and then continue on, eventually earning a bachelor's degree in plastics engineering technology.

For information, write to Plastics Engineering Technology Program, Plastics Building, Room 104, Big Rapids, Michigan 49307.

Georgia Institute of Technology

Within the College of Engineering, Georgia Institute of Technology offers a multidisciplinary, bachelor's degree program in plastics engineering—the production, characterization, and application of polymeric materials.

Through the apply-by-computer program, anyone with access to a computer terminal and a modem can submit an undergraduate application for admission via the Georgia Tech computer network. The system also lets prospective students submit co-op applications, request data on the institute, and monitor the status of their application.

The M.S. and Ph.D. degrees in polymer science are offered by the School of Chemical Engineering. Within the School of Chemical Engineering, multidisciplinary programs at the graduate level include the Polymer Program, the Composites Program, and the Computer Integrated Manufacturing Systems (CIMS) Program. Students use laboratories and equipment at The Polymer Education and Research Center, and they have opportunities for collaborative research with colleagues at the Georgia Tech Research Institute, also on the Georgia Tech campus.

For information, write to Georgia Institute of Technology, Atlanta, Georgia 30332-0100.

Illinois Institute of Technology

At Illinois Institute of Technology, a private coeducational university in Chicago, undergraduates interested in polymer science will find courses offered by more than one department. The Metallurgical and Materials Engineering Department has a course in plastic working, which includes rolling, forging, extruding, and other forming processes. The Chemical Engineering Department offers a professional specialization in polymer chemistry, characterization, structure, and properties; the manufacture of polymeric raw materials; and the processing of such raw materials into finished products.

At the graduate level, the Illinois Institute of Technology has a master's degree program in metallurgical and materials engineering, designed for employed professionals who go to school parttime. The department offers a specialization in polymer science and engineering, in conjunction with the Departments of Chemical Engineering and Chemistry.

At the Ph.D. level, course work in various polymer topics is available: structure and properties of polymers and theory of mechanical behavior of polymers are examples. A course on commercial polymers explains properties, structure, and processing methods for commercially important thermoplastics and thermosets, and provides information on foamed and fiber-reinforced plastics.

For information, write to Illinois Institute of Technology, IIT Center, 3300 South Federal Street, Chicago, Illinois 60616-3793.

The Pennsylvania State University

Penn State offers polymer science courses leading to the B.S., M.S., and Ph.D. degrees. At the undergraduate level, students have general education requirements in social and behavioral sciences, arts, and humanities. In addition, 79 credits of prescribed courses are required; these include chemistry, physics, math, statistics, and materials science, as well as specific courses in polymer science. Students also take 15 credits of supporting courses (technical electives), nine credits of which must be in a logical sequence. Penn State requires students to earn a 2.0 or better grade point average in courses required for their major.

Penn State, which offers both M.S. and Ph.D. degrees in polymer science, considers the Ph.D. primarily a research degree. The university advises the combination of an M.S. degree and industrial experience for those who intend to pursue careers in industrial operations or development, rather than fundamental research. A master's degree plus job experience, Penn State says, may represent a more effective background than equivalent time spent obtaining a Ph.D.

Penn State's Polymer Science Club is an active student organization that sponsors a variety of professional and social activities. The school also has special facilities for research in polymer synthesis, polymer blends, surface science, mechanical properties, modeling and theoretical studies, diffraction and scattering, multicomponent systems, polymer characterization, high temperature stable polymers, optical and STEM microscopy, vibrational spectroscopy, and thermal analysis.

For more information, write to the Polymer Science Program, Department of Materials Science and Engineering, College of Earth and Mineral Sciences, 320 Steidle Building, The Pennsylvania State University, University Park, Pennsylvania 16802.

Rutgers University

At Rutgers, the State University of New Jersey, the graduate program in materials science and engineering offers the degrees of Master of Science and Doctor of Philosophy. The program emphasizes the relationships between the microscopic structure and macroscopic properties of materials. All students take common core courses to strengthen their academic foundation; they can then specialize in either physical metallurgy or polymer science.

Polymer science courses are concerned with the theoretical and experimental study of molecular structure, crystal structure and morphology, and molecular motion. Students also study the relationship of these topics to the macroscopic properties of polymers.

For information, write to the Department of Mechanics and Materials Science, Rutgers, the State University of New Jersey, P.O. Box 909, Piscataway, New Jersey 08855.

Also at Rutgers: an applied sciences in engineering curriculum with a packaging engineering option. This program prepares scientists and engineers for a major role in the complex and challenging field of packaging. Structural package design is only one part of packaging engineering; the field also involves materials science and engineering, machinery design and use, manufacturing methods, packaging regulations, marketing, economics, and product distribution. In courses on package manufacturing processes, students study manufacturing methods for glass, metal, plastic, and paper; they also observe these methods on field trips. In the packaging materials course, students discuss structure, properties, and materials. They explore design from a consumer safety point of view. Solid waste disposal and recycling of packaging materials are also covered.

For information about the B.S. program and the packaging engineering option, write to the Coordinator, Undergraduate Packaging Engineering Program, College of Engineering, Rutgers, the State University of New Jersey, Building 3529, Busch Campus, Piscataway, New Jersey 08855.

University of Akron

Home of the Polymer Hall of Fame, the University of Akron has been prominent in polymer research and studies since 1910, when it offered its first course in rubber chemistry. Today, its College of Polymer Science and Polymer Engineering (created in 1988) consists of the Department of Polymer Science, the Department of Polymer Engineering, the Institute of Polymer Science, and the Center for Polymer Engineering.

The Department of Polymer Science offers master's and doctoral degrees for students with backgrounds in the physical sciences and engineering. Study areas focus on the synthesizing of new polymers and their physical and mechanical properties. The Department of Polymer Engineering, which offers a graduate program leading to an M.S. in polymer engineering, emphasizes the properties, processing and performance of polymers. Its doctoral program emphasizes research in polymer processing and applications.

The Center for Polymer Engineering, which has state-of-the-art processing equipment and laboratories, concentrates on the applications of new polymer technologies and materials. The University of Akron, along with Case Western Reserve University (Cleveland, Ohio), also participates in the Edison Polymer Innovation Corporation (EPIC), which includes more than 70 corporations and community members from the Akron/Cleveland area. Together, the academic and business sectors develop new polymer technologies, processes, and products.

For information on courses, write to the College of Polymer Science and Polymer Engineering, The University of Akron, Akron, Ohio 44325-3909. For information on Edison Polymer Innovation Corporation (EPIC), write to 3505 East Royalton Road, Broadview Heights, Ohio 44147.

University of Lowell

Plastics Engineering has been taught for nearly 40 years at The University of Lowell, ever since a university committee discovered plastics was one of the most rapidly growing industries in Massachusetts. Today, Lowell offers a bachelor's, master's, and doctoral degree in plastics engineering, as well as a Ph.D. program in chemistry with an option in polymer science/plastics engineering.

Undergraduates in Lowell's plastics engineering program receive hands-on laboratory training in all aspects of mold making and molding, as well as basic and engineering sciences, with an emphasis on polymers. The plastics industry recruits and competes aggressively for Lowell graduates; the school has a 100 percent placement record.

At University of Lowell, the M.S. program provides an opportunity for the study of theory and practice in plastics. If desired, the fiber/composite materials option prepares master's degree candidates for careers in the reinforced plastics and advanced composite materials industries.

The Doctor of Engineering degree in plastics engineering produces professionals qualified for technical management positions in the plastics industry as well as for administrative positions in government, and teaching careers in colleges and universities. A one-year internship in industry, government, or at the university is required—placing the student in a setting in which he or she functions as a high-level engineer.

The Institute for Plastics Innovation at Lowell focuses on building a comprehensive plastics manufacturing program through institute-initiated research, educational and training services, technology transfer programs, consulting, and contract research services. Its applied research program coordinates existing technology in the areas of product design, materials research and development, processing technology, and machinery and equipment development—all specific to the plastics manufacturing process.

For information, write to the University of Lowell, Plastics Engineering Department, One University Avenue, Lowell, Massachusetts 01854.

Western Washington University

Within the program leading to a major in industrial technology, students at this Bellingham, Washington, school can specialize in plastics technology—with courses that include reinforced plastics/composites, tooling for plastics processing, polymer chemistry, injection molding, industrial quality assurance, polymer formulation and analysis, and numerical control operations. Students also are required to take 70 credits of core courses: chemistry, calculus and physics, financial accounting, and materials technology are among them.

For information, write to Department of Technology, Western Washington University, Bellingham, Washington 98225.

SEMINARS

An excellent way to receive training in plastics technology is to enroll in special industry seminars. Often, they're taught by one of the industry associations and given at various locations around the country. For instance, the Society of Plastics Engineers offers seminars in Atlanta, Baltimore, Montreal, Chicago, Denver, Stamford (Connecticut), Indianapolis, Dallas, and St. Louis.

These are typical seminar titles throughout the year: Injection Molding, Injection Mold Tooling Technology, A Designer's Guide to Part Design for Economical Injection Molding, Production Injection Molding Manufacturing Techniques, Phasing Computer-Aided Engineering Into Injection Molding Operations, Plastics in Automotives—A Showcase, Thermoforming Technology for Industrial Applications, Extrusion of Polymers, Extrusion Principles and Practices, Die Design Principles for Extrusion of Polymers, and An Applications Engineering Review of Plastic Materials and Processes.

Although course content in these seminars is typically intensive, instructors know they're lecturing to a broad-based audience, not just to hands-on engineers. The seminar on injection molding, for example, is designed to provide a working knowledge of injection molding technology to marketing, production, sales, management, and technical personnel. The molding machine, the injection mold, the theory of plastic flow and its practical applications, and examples of molded parts are systematically examined. The seminar is designed to help participants solve the problems of designing, manufacturing, and selling injection molded parts.

The seminar titled ''An Applications Engineering Review of Plastic Materials and Processes'' is aimed at applications, design, manufacturing, purchasing, and sales engineers—offering them a working knowledge of plastic materials and fabrication processes. The plastics used, the tooling required, and the capabilities and limitations for each of 112 processing techniques are reviewed—with a summary of major markets, share, and growth trends given for each of the processing techniques.

For the beginning student in plastics technology, or someone who's merely considering a career, the cost of attending such a seminar, including travel, may seem high. Most seminars cost $400–$800. Nevertheless, they can provide you with a quick insight into the complexities of plastics. You'll know from your reaction to several intensive days of speeches, and the handout materials, whether you really *enjoy* the field, and want to continue learning about it. Often, too, society membership fees are included in the nonmember registration fee.

For information on seminars offered by SPE, write to Society of Plastics Engineers, 14 Fairfield Drive, Brookfield, Connecticut 06804.

Since seminar costs are substantially less for society members, it usually pays to join the particular society before registering for a seminar.

SME Seminars

The Society of Manufacturing Engineers (SME) is another association that offers seminars in technical subjects—some dealing with plastics. A typical seminar is CAD/CAM (Computer-Aided Design, Computer-Aided Manufacturing) Technology for the Design of Molds for the Plastics Molding Industry. This comprehensive two-day clinic helps improve the accuracy and timeliness of mold design.

Other recent offerings have included Resin Transfer Molding for the Aerospace Industry and Resin Transfer Molding for the Automotive Industry.

Another course SME has offered, Plastics Technology: An Introduction to the Nature and Use of Plastic Material, covers technology useful in understanding plastics structures and properties. Those who attend—primarily product development engineers, process engineers, design engineers, material engineers, and quality control personnel—learn how to select and evaluate materials for plastics applications.

For information on seminars, contact the Society of Manufacturing Engineers, Courses & Clinics Department, One SME Drive, P.O. Box 930, Dearborn, Michigan 48121-0930.

The Plastics Institute of America offers various courses—some, in-house—to managers involved with plastics in their business operations, experienced polymer technicians, or those in research and development, design, engineering, manufacturing, and quality control. Courses have included Plastics Injection Molding Manufacturing Techniques, Plastics Extrusion Manufacturing Techniques, Principles of Polymer Science and Technology,

Polymer Testing and Characterization, and Plastics Processing Technology Workshop. Courses on plastics recycling technology also are taught. Additional information is available from the Plastics Institute of America, Inc., Suite 100, 277 Fairfield Road, Fairfield, New Jersey 07004-1932.

Other Seminars

Workshops and seminars on more general engineering topics are also offered by the Institute of Industrial Engineers. Such seminars concentrate on the design, installation, and maintenance of integrated systems of resources, and on the latest trends and developments in various industries. For more information, write to the Institute of Industrial Engineers, 25 Technology Park, P.O. Box 6150, Norcross, Georgia 30091-6150.

CHAPTER 4

FINANCING YOUR EDUCATION

START EARLY

There are a number of ways you can cut down the cost of receiving training to work in the plastics industry. How effective any of them will be for you depends a great deal on your personal efforts. Grades count when you're applying for scholarships and grants. So does a good record in extracurricular activities, especially in activities that are related to the course of study you hope to pursue. It's possible that a plastics company near you may sponsor an Explorer Scout post, or that your high school or community college has a club for future engineers. Ask questions. Find out what's available, join, and, if possible, take a leadership role. Not only will you learn about engineering and technology, but you'll demonstrate to those who look at financial applications that you're serious about your future career.

Junior Engineering Technical Society (JETS)

One society you may want to contact is the Junior Engineering Technical Society (JETS)—a nationwide organization for precollege students interested in engineering, technology, mathematics, and science. JETS offers a number of activities, including TEAMS (Tests of Engineering Aptitude, Math and Science). TEAMS is an academic competition with local, state, and national awards that identifies outstanding groups of students who succeed, both because they have attained high academic ability and because they work well together. The TEAMS competition exam covers six subject areas: biology, chemistry, computer fundamentals, English, mathematics, and physics. High school teams work together in an open-book, open-note, open-discussion format to answer the test questions.

JETS also sponsors the National Engineering Aptitude Search (NEAS), a guidance-oriented examination for high school students considering careers in engineering, mathematics, science, or technology. Though the NEAS does not predict whether students will become successful engineers, the exam helps determine their strengths and weaknesses. The NEAS consists of two different tests. Students are encouraged to take the NEAS in 9th or 10th grade to help them identify courses they should take in high school to improve their chances for success in a college-level engineering, math, science, or technology program. Students also take the test in 11th or 12th grade for additional testing experience and to verify their level of mathematical and scientific preparedness for college.

Another JETS program, National Engineering Design Challenge, teaches students real-life applications for engineering concepts when they design and build a product to address a specific need. Topics have included designing and producing a working model of a device that would replace a highway construction flagperson, and designing a page-turner for a multiple-handicapped person. Each team works with an engineer who advises them throughout the project.

To find out more about JETS, write to the Junior Engineering Technical Society (JETS), 345 East 47th Street, New York, New York, 10017.

Work Experience

The work record you build while in school is also evaluated when you apply for scholarships, loans, or grants. You'll almost certainly be asked for references, and you want to provide good ones. Dependability, reliability, willingness to work as part of a team, and a performance track record an employer can depend on count as pluses.

Dr. Roger D. Corneliussen, professor of materials engineering at Drexel University, gives this advice:

> Start your work experience in the field early. Look for companies that make plastics or plastics products. Virtually every section of the country has small companies that do injection molding or thermoforming. Get a job there, even if you're sweeping the floors. You'll be surprised at how much you'll learn, and how much the knowledge you absorb will help you later.

Once you have the extracurricular and work experience you need, your high school or community college guidance office is a good place to start looking for financial aid. They will have names and addresses of places you should contact. Write, too, to the schools to which you're applying for admission. Since funds are limited, begin your search as soon as possible.

Write to the American College Testing Program, P.O. Box 168, Iowa City, Iowa 52243 for a free copy of *Applying for Financial Aid: Financial Aid Services*. It's updated annually. Write to the College Board, College Board Publications, Box 2815, Princeton, New Jersey 08541 for similar free material.

TMA APPRENTICESHIPS

One way of financing your post–high school training for the plastics industry is to enter an apprentice training program. A formal industry apprenticeship, as defined by the U.S. Department of Labor's Bureau of Apprenticeship and Training, must consist of four or five years of on-the-job training supplemented by related theory classes. In the Chicago metropolitan area, such a program exists—sponsored by the Tooling & Manufacturing Association. This regional trade association serves approximately 1,500 precision metalworking firms in the six northeastern Illinois counties that make up the Chicago metropolitan area.

Some of their member companies do plastics molding. Moldmakers, also called precision metalworkers, build highly engineered molds out of hardened steel. The molds are then set up into mold presses to produce component plastic parts for many of the products we use daily.

In addition, precision metalworking professionals design and make the tools, dies, molds, die cast dies, and special machines used in virtually all mass production. They also machine high-precision component parts. Production workers then stamp, mold, fabricate, cast, forge, turn, bend, machine, and grind precision parts used by end-product manufacturers.

For nearly sixty years, TMA has been helping member companies train their apprentices. Each year TMA's related theory program enrolls an average of 700 to 800 apprentices; approximately 200 graduate each year from the three-year program. While apprentices can't enroll in classes on their own, they are eligible to enroll as soon as they've been hired by a TMA member. TMA has a free referral service that individuals may use to find employment with member companies. It's available to anyone who isn't already working for a TMA member company.

Those who would like to use the referral service must make an appointment with TMA's education department, since job information cannot be sent through the mail. Instead, applicants come to TMA's offices and copy the job openings out of the referral book.

TMA recommends strongly that job seekers have a typed resume ready, which will be placed in the association's "applicant available" book. An outline of relevant courses students have taken—such as math, shop, drafting, electronics, computers, and other technical courses—is an essential part of an employer's evaluation of a potential apprentice. The greater an applicant's training or experience in the metalworking trades, the easier it will be to get an apprenticeship. Someone with no technical background will find it difficult to get an apprenticeship.

TMA has apprentice training programs for tool and die makers, moldmakers, machinists, and sheet-metal/modelmakers. TMA courses are approved for college credit at the three suburban Chicagoland campuses TMA uses for classes: College of DuPage, Triton College, and Oakton Community College. Apprentices can transfer TMA credits between any of the three campuses.

The TMA brochure "How Valuable Is Your Future?" compares the annual income of a tool and die maker with that of a mechanical engineer over a twelve-year period. On a year-by-year basis, TMA says, tool and die makers earn while they learn, while student engineers remain in debt until they find a job after graduation. At the end of six years, a tool and die maker has accumulated over $178,296 in income (annual amounts vary from case to case, of course), while a mechanical engineer has earned $39,450. The association says that the $138,846 differential is an important consideration in planning career alternatives.

For more information, write to the Tooling & Manufacturing Association, 1177 South Dee Road, Park Ridge, Illinois 60068–9809.

Financing Your Education 45

SCHOLARSHIPS

Students with good to excellent grade point averages, leadership abilities, and a record of extracurricular activities stand the best chance of earning a scholarship. Many scholarships are based on financial need; others, however, are not.

Listed below are some of the best-known scholarships being offered. Contact the organizations listed below—and your guidance counselor—for more detailed information and application forms. You'll find additional listings, specifically for women and minorities, in Chapter 13 of this book. Check your library or counseling office, too, for a copy of *Directory of Financial Aids for Minorities,* a biennial book by Gail Ann Schlachter (Reference Service Press).

National Merit Scholarship

The National Merit Scholarship program is the largest and most widely known private scholarship for undergraduate study, offering college money to several thousand of the nation's most outstanding students each year. The sum total of National Merit $2,000 scholarship awards reaches over $3.6 million annually. Corporate- and college-sponsored scholarships given to National Merit finalists exceeded $17 million in 1985.

More than a million high school students enter the program each year when they take the Preliminary Scholastic Aptitude Test/National Merit Scholarship Qualifying Test (PSAT/NMSQT). Only the students who represent the upper half of one percent of high school graduates in each state are selected as semifinalists, and thereby become eligible to continue in the competition for scholarship opportunities.

For information, write to the National Merit Scholarship Corporation, One Rotary Center, Evanston, Illinois 60201.

NSPE Educational Foundation

The National Society of Professional Engineers Educational Foundation, NPSE Information Center, 1420 King Street, Alexandria, Virginia 22314–2715, awards more than a million dollars annually in engineering scholarships. The awards vary from $1,000 for one year to full tuition for four years. Scholarships are given to high school students who rank in the top one-fourth of their class. Students must be U.S. citizens and must plan to continue the study of engineering at a college or university with an engineering curriculum in the pertinent branch accredited by the Accreditation Board for Engineering & Technology (ABET).

Westinghouse Science Talent Search

Since 1942, this nationwide competition had identified and encouraged high school seniors to pursue careers in science, mathematics, or related fields. In that time, nearly 105,000 students have completed independent research projects and submitted entries. Currently, some 1,500 seniors meet the entry requirements each year—requirements that consist of a written description of the student's research plus a completed entry form providing evidence of student creativity and interest in science.

The top 300 entrants, selected as semifinalists, are recommended to colleges and universities for admission and financial assistance, based on their STS achievement. Forty finalists receive a 5-day trip to Washington for interviews. A total of $205,000 is awarded each year to the 40 finalists. The top prize is a $40,000 scholarship.

Five former finalists have gone on to win Nobel Prizes. Two have earned Fields Medals, the Nobel equivalent in math. Two have been awarded the National Medal of Science. Eight Search alumni have won MacArthur Foundation Fellowships; fifty-one have been named Sloan Research Fellows, and twenty-eight have

Financing Your Education 47

been elected to the National Academy of Sciences. Three have been elected to the National Academy of Engineering.

For information, rules, and entry blank, write to the Westinghouse Science Talent Search, c/o Science Service, 1719 N Street, NW, Washington, D.C. 20036.

COOPERATIVE PROGRAMS

Earning while you learn is also possible with engineering co-op programs, offered at a number of the schools and colleges mentioned in Chapter 3 of this book. In a typical cooperative program, usually available to students after their freshman year, students alternate a semester on campus with a semester on-site with a sponsoring company. If you choose this option, you will be paid while you work, and your performance will be watched closely. You will work under the guidance and supervision of experienced professionals and get a sense of what the working world is like and what challenges workers face. Roger A. Corneliussen, editor of *Drexel Polymer Notes* and professor of materials engineering at Drexel University says, "Sometimes coop students actually solve technical problems that the more experienced professionals haven't because [the students] look at [problems] with a fresh approach."

In general, it takes longer to complete an engineering co-op program than a regular program. Drexel's co-op program takes five years. But co-op students usually find more career opportunities than their non-co-oping classmates.

Several inexpensive publications listing cooperative programs are available from various organizations. Write to Accreditation Board for Engineering and Technology (ABET), 345 East 47th Street, New York, New York 10017, for *Accredited Programs Leading to Degrees In Engineering, By Institution*. This material includes schools whose cooperative programs are accredited by ABET.

Write to National Commission for Cooperative Education, 360 Huntington Avenue, Boston, Massachusetts 02115, for *Undergraduate Programs of Cooperative Education in the United States and Canada.*

Write to CED Directory, P.O. Box M, Mississippi State, Mississippi 39762, for *Engineering Co-op Directory,* a complete directory of all co-op engineering in the United States and Canada.

SUMMER WORK

If you're a good student and well-recommended by your professors, your school placement office may be able to help you find a summer job in plastics or a related field. Manny Panos, placement director at the University of Lowell (a Massachusetts school which set up its plastics engineering program in 1954), says that in summer, 1990, ''I had two students from the program working in Irvine, California; three in San Francisco; three in Texas; and two in New Orleans.''

In short, there's no easy way to meet the high cost of education and training, but a creative search for financial aid can help. Don't be afraid to demonstrate the skills, ability, and characteristics for success that you possess.

CHAPTER 5

PERSONAL QUALITIES

What personal qualities are necessary to do well in the plastics industry? Who succeeds in this expanding field?

TEAMWORK

Interpersonal skills are near the top of the list. Plastics veterans feel that the ability to work with others is essential. They stress the ability to get along in a team environment, to be willing to adjust, to make a real contribution. Wherever you work—for an international fiber-producing company or at a small fabricating firm that buys preformed plastics and turns them into consumer products—you need the human relations skills to get along.

Organizations are beginning to stress teamwork as part of company culture. A good example is the Hoechst Group, a German-based international firm whose products include polymers, fibers, and plastic film. Since half of the group is employed outside Germany, the company's goal of achieving a greater international division of labor within the company will necessitate close cooperation among people of different cultures.

AUTONOMY

Also valued is the ability to work independently and responsibly. Monsanto Chemical Company, which produces such products as synthetic fibers, plastics, resins, and thermoplastic alloys, places strong emphasis on self-management. "This means," the company says, "you're encouraged to take initiative, seek answers on your own, and challenge the status quo. Independent thinkers flourish in this kind of environment. But independence is only half of the equation—we need people who can also effectively solve problems as part of a team."

ENTHUSIASM

"Go to work and love your job and find a better way to do it!" suggests Henry Tschappat, director of the plastics program at Ferris State University. "There's a real shortage of dedicated, skilled craftspeople. You'll be noticed."

"We like to see people come in with a can-do attitude," concurs K. R. Davis, manager of human resources for Hoechst Group's plant in Bishop, Texas.

RESPONSIBLE BEHAVIOR

Take your schoolwork seriously. "If you're going to help young people with this book," says Monroe Miller, with the Houston-based executive search firm of Ryman, Bell, Green and Michaels, "they need to know they began their career when they started their schooling. A bad school record will hinder you for the rest of your life. Our clients look for grade point averages of 3.0 or better."

Outside the classroom, responsible behavior is just as crucial. Though companies may not choose to publicize it, more and more are doing drug screening as part of a required pre-employment physical. "I tell candidates about this," says Patrick Layhee of M. David Lowe Personnel, a large independently-owned personnel service in the Southwest. "I say, 'Is this a problem?' Some do call me back and decline an interview."

COMMITMENT TO LEARNING

In the high-tech world of a modern chemical company, growing personally and professionally takes continuous education and training. Companies expect you to take advantage of opportunities, which they often initiate. For instance, Union Carbide Chemicals and Plastics, the worldwide chemicals and plastics business of Union Carbide, has established a continuing education center that offers employees a range of career and self-development courses centered on the company's "Excellence through Quality" program—defined as a "do it right the first time" effort.

Ideally, your commitment to learning should be lifelong. A 39-year-old father of three at one of Ciba-Geigy's Swiss factories puts it this way:

> After a few months there, I was able to start the three-year course for skilled chemical process workers—at full pay, I'm happy to say, because by then I was married and had three children. I qualified and worked for four years in production. Then I was accepted for the chargehands' course. During thirty days of instruction spread over half a year, we immersed ourselves in what it takes to lead a team. We also got to know a fair amount about the company: its history, its present-day scope, and what it aims to be in future. The candidate foreman's course I am now on is even more demanding.

It runs for a whole year and takes about 90 working days to complete. A third of the course time is devoted to specialized training in chemistry, physics, and the German language. Again, though, the emphasis is on leadership, involving technical aspects such as planning, organization, instruction, and control; and "people" aspects such as communication, motivation, and health.

TECHNICAL SAVVY—AND A LOT MORE

Here's how Monsanto sums up its goals:

"In addition to strong capability in your specific area of expertise, we look for superior leadership skills, good decision making, sound judgment, and vision. In other words, we want people who hunger for more than just a job. We want people who are determined to make a difference."

CHAPTER 6

FINDING A JOB

One of the country's most successful placement programs for new plastics engineers is run by the University of Lowell, which has placed 100 percent of its new graduates in the last seven years. "We don't have enough graduates to go around," says Manny Panos, director of the university's career planning and placement office.

In 1990, 68 companies recruited plastics engineers on campus, he says, but more than a hundred companies wanted to come. Those that did included Baxter-Travenol, General Motors, General Electric, Du Pont, Dow Chemical, IBM, Monsanto, Tupperware, Owens-Corning, and Xerox—"all the heavyweights," as Panos puts it. Each of the 50 or 60 students Lowell graduates in plastics engineering at the bachelor's level generally has ten to thirteen on-campus interviews and a nationwide pick of jobs, with an average entry-level salary of $33,270 and a range of $31,200 to $34,500. Those graduating with master's degrees average $38,130 with a range of $35,000 to $41,400.

Panos says he also released graduates' resumes to an additional 60 companies. Each day he receives two or three calls from "headhunters" (employment search firms) looking for Lowell students and alumni. Though the university's impressive track record may be unusual—some say that specialty and commodity plastics are depressed businesses—Panos makes the odds better for recent graduates by training them in the job-hunting process. His tips are worth following; they have proven effective.

START EARLY

Students should start their search for a job *before* graduation—no later than the beginning of their junior year in college, Panos says. He suggests students find part-time work, internships, and summer jobs that will look good on their resumes. Panos also recommends that students run for office in a campus organization to demonstrate leadership.

Co-op spots help give students valuable background and industry contacts. So do summer jobs. If you want to work in plastics, Panos advises, make sure you're exposed to the industry between your junior and senior years. Even if you take a job on the second shift in a plant, working only four hours a day, you've picked up a valuable credential. Your placement office can help you get summer jobs, Panos says, even if they may be far from home.

For instance, though the University of Lowell is in Massachusetts, Panos found summer jobs for five student plastics engineers in California (two in Irvine, three in San Francisco), three in Texas, and two in New Orleans.

DO YOUR HOMEWORK

During the year, on campus, Panos runs daily workshops on placement for three weeks straight, urging students to get serious about job hunting. In these three-hour workshops, Panos talks about professional societies (in plastics, the Society of Plastics

Engineers, the Society of the Plastics Industry) and suggests they join student chapters. He encourages students to read trade and business publications—especially the *Wall Street Journal*—and to talk frequently with their professors and advisors about career goals.

"Be mobile," he says. "If you want to stay close to home, you'll limit your opportunities. You may need to move to a different part of the country; it's easier right after graduation than it is if you've got kids and half a house paid for."

His recommendation: consider job hunting as a college course. "For every three-credit course, you'd do two hours of homework for each hour spent in class," he says. "That's nine hours a week. You should be spending the full nine hours each and every week on your career plans, doing your personal preparation."

That "study time," Panos says, should include thoroughly reading and analyzing the last two quarterly reports of companies in the industry. "If you know how to read numbers and can zero in on the division which may be interviewing you," he says, "your knowledge will be evident during the interview and will show you've done your homework."

Reading reports also gives students a feel for the company culture—a "fit" the interviewer will look for. "You need to know how your motivation and interpersonal skills will match the philosophy and direction of a company," Panos says.

Panos also trains students in telephone interviewing and reviews cover letters before students send them.

He and Dr. Nick R. Schott, director of Lowell's plastics program, believe the plastics industry will provide even more opportunities in the coming years. Schott says:

> Plastics is growing at a rate two to three times that of our national economy. It's a more competitive method of manufacturing. Plastics are winning out over other materials, including metals, glass, ceramics, or paper, because of the

cost of manufacturing and the cost of energy. Opportunities exist in almost every state—and because plastics as an industry is still growing, there are more opportunities in plastics than there are in more mature industries.

TRADE JOURNALS

Reading the "trades" (see periodicals list in Appendix A) is another good way to determine what types of jobs may be available in the plastics industry. Trade journals will help you learn what qualifications potential employers want and what salary ranges they may offer. (Salaries, of course, vary by region.)

Often, listings in the classified section of the trades give information on jobs offered through agencies. For instance, a recent listing in *Plastics World* advertised jobs for high-speed packaging engineers, form/fill/seal engineers, heat sealing/foil/plastics engineers, blow molding engineers, and polymer chemists. Another ad offered jobs in tech service for urethanes ($30,000 to $45,000), market development for engineering resins ($37,000 to $47,000), and supervisors of injection molding ($25,000).

One typical ad in *Modern Plastics* described jobs for plastics engineers in the production of polycarbonate prescription lenses, a fast-growing segment of the eye glass lens industry. Another ad was for a plastics engineer for a foamed plastics company to provide manufacturing plastics technical support for ongoing operations and implementation of new products, from research and development to production scale, including formulation, extrusion, and compounding. This position required a minimum of three years of relevant experience and a B.S. or M.S. degree in plastics engineering. A third ad was for a quality control manager for a thermoplastic injection molding plant in Michigan.

Packaging Digest carried ads for a sales executive in plastic packaging, with a minimum of five years' experience in selling six-color printed poly bags; a Midwest salesperson for 8-ounce to 36-ounce plastic bottles manufactured primarily for the private label market or custom market; and a southeastern representative for a plastic printing and converting operation.

USING A PERSONNEL SERVICE

M. David Lowe

Patrick Layhee is professional group manager with M. David Lowe, one of the largest personnel services in Texas. The 33-year-old firm places administrative and professional candidates in a variety of fields.

"Engineers who are recent graduates are in high demand," says Layhee. "We have job orders from our clients, and can get [recent grads] interviews. In plastics and petrochemicals, companies are looking for chemical and mechanical engineers."

Most candidates for employment his agency sees come from the Gulf Coast area, Layhee says, because of the concentration of petrochemical manufacturing within a hundred miles of Houston. "If we have candidates that already live here, it's easier for a company to hire them for jobs," he explains. "Then the company doesn't have to worry about whether a candidate has to sell a house or drag the kids out of school and move."

The agency contacts campuses to learn of promising seniors. In addition, the agency may learn of experienced candidates because it has previously placed their friends. M. David Lowe also maintains a computerized bank of applicants who have registered with them over the years.

All placement fees are paid by the hiring company, Layhee says. "Because companies pay the fees, applicants have an incentive to come to us," he explains. "We can come up with no-obligation interviews. We call applicants and present companies that want to interview them."

Most marketable in plastics and petrochemicals, he says, are applicants on their first or second job change. "Employers like to see engineers on the way up," he explains. "They've trained on someone else's payroll. They've matured professionally."

Entry-level salaries for recent chemical engineering graduates with a bachelor's degree, Layhee says, average $3,100 a month. A mechanical engineer with a bachelor's degree from a school comparable to Texas A&M may start at $2,950 a month. Candidates who are recruited through college placement offices get the highest salaries—that's because it's expensive to recruit on campus. Usually, Layhee says, companies who do are among the Fortune 1,000, like Exxon and Texaco, and they are paying "top dollar for the cream of the crop."

SKILLS AND QUALIFICATIONS

Layhee says companies base their hiring decisions on skills and qualifications. "All things being equal," he says, "if you had two recent graduates who were chemical engineers and one had worked at Burger King while the other had engineering co-op experience, the person who'd been in the manufacturing plant would get hired first and would be offered a higher salary."

Also important to companies looking for experienced personnel: stable tenure and *focused* careers. "Don't be a generalist," Layhee advises. "Don't say on a resume, 'I'm an experienced manager.' Instead, say, 'I am a plastics expert.' " Companies hire specialists, he says. "They want to know what skills you bring to the table . . . what focus you have. Can you hit the ground running? They pay us to get quality."

RESUME FORMATS

Layhee has specific resume-writing advice. "It's not an all-encompassing bio," he says. "They won't read a long resume. Its purpose is to get the company to contact you."

Books that suggest a functional resume based on a summary of your experience are wrong, Layhee says, because companies want facts, not vague summaries. Companies think you have something to hide, especially if there's a gap in dates:

> I tell applicants, "Whatever you did in that gap is not as bad as what the employer will think. It's ok to tell them you were out of work, if that's what happened."
>
> List your experience from your degree right up to the present, and do it by month and year. Don't just put 1981–1982 and 1983–1986. You could have been out of work nearly two years during that period, if your job ended in January 1982, and you didn't start the next one until December 1983. The correct format should be: dates you were with the company, company name, your title, brief list of responsibilities and accomplishments.
>
> Say, "references provided on request," rather than listing names. Include where you went to school, the field in which you got your degree, and date of graduation.

A must for resumes, Layhee feels, is a daytime phone number. "Visualize a human resources manager at 10:30 A.M. They see your resume. They want to pick up the phone and reach you. If you've given your home number and you have an answering machine, don't have Billy Idol or heavy metal playing."

HANDLING INTERVIEWS

The purpose of a job interview is to get an offer, Layhee says. But some applicants don't see it that way. "They get a first call and get invited for the interview," he says. "Maybe the job is in

Kentucky, and they don't want to go. Take the interview. If you get an offer, you can always turn it down."

Applicants' conduct during the interview is important, too. "Questions like 'What's the job like?,' 'What projects are involved?,' 'Who will be my boss?' are legitimate questions, but don't ask them first. Employers hire people who want to get up and go to work. They want people who are sold on the job."

Acceptable reasons for job changing, Layhee points out, don't really include, "I want more challenge and opportunity." That's too vague. Companies prefer answers like these.

- We have new management. They're going to bring in their own team.
- Company profits are down.
- I want a supervisory role. I'm blocked out; my boss is 35.
- I need more technical projects.

"All those are okay," Layhee says. "Vagueness turns people off. Having a good, focused reason for changing jobs helps. Also, don't have too broad an objective on your resume. You can say, 'I'm interested in process engineering,' but put that on a cover sheet, rather than in your resume."

Layhee advises applicants to use what he terms "high touch."

"If you have a good-looking resume with plenty of white space, put a brief hand-written note on top, saying, 'Please call me if you're interested.' " As part of its marketing and personal promotion, Layhee's agency hand-addresses envelopes, using blue ink and white paper. "They get opened by client companies first," Layhee says.

His advice: "Consider your career as a marathon, not a 100-yard dash. Pace yourself. Don't feel you have to make a million right now. You're going to be working for a number of years. Don't make job changes too quickly. Be operations-oriented, rather than money-oriented. The money will come."

During interviews, Layhee suggests, candidates should ask for an offer. His advice to young professionals: "Don't just tell a prospective employer you can do the job; instead, say you'd like to have the position, even though you may feel uncomfortable with that wording. Companies like people who like them."

Layhee suggests following up interviews with hand-written notes to each person you met. It's easier to remember names and titles, he says, if you get a business card from each person. The tone of the note should be something like, "Thank you for the interview. I think I have the skills to do your job. I don't see any reason why we can't get together. I hope to hear from you soon."

Ryman, Bell, Green and Michaels

Monroe Miller is an associate with Ryman, Bell, Green and Michaels, an executive search firm in Houston, Texas, that works internationally on a contract basis with clients in various industries, including plastics/petrochemicals and pharmaceuticals. The firm keeps a file of names of personnel already working in the field, Miller says. Although it sometimes markets a particular candidate, the firm primarily concentrates on filling client companies' requests. Fees are paid by the firm's clients, rather than by candidates.

"Generally, we're called in when newspaper ads and referrals haven't worked for a client," he says. "Most often, the vacancies are positions that have to be filled with candidates who have very specific characteristics. We receive explicit job descriptions from our clients."

The first step towards a possible "match" comes when Ryman, Bell, Green and Michaels contacts people listed in its files who seem to have ability and experience the client has specified.

PRESCREENING

"In this phone prescreening, we explain the job description," Miller says. "We tell possible candidates all that we understand about the financial history, financial position, and market share of the client company. We try to determine whether there's a potential fit between a candidate's background and our client's needs."

Likely candidates—who aren't told what or where the potential job opening is during the firm's phone prescreening—are asked to send a resume to Ryman, Bell, Green and Michaels. "Once we've evaluated the resume and determined the fit, we get back to them, explain the opportunity, and determine if they're really interested," Miller says.

Some candidates are willing to relocate. Others aren't. Often money isn't the problem; family needs such as a working spouse, children finishing high school, or aging parents may make qualified candidates unwilling to go further in the hiring process.

Ryman, Bell, Green and Michaels doesn't initially pass candidates' resumes directly to the client. Instead, the firm summarizes the candidate's background for the client, and, if the client is interested, forwards the resume.

Important to clients, Miller says, is the candidate's grade point average. Ryman, Bell, Green and Michaels looks for a GPA of 3.0 or better. The firm has traditionally placed candidates with bachelor's degrees, but client companies are beginning to specify graduate work or a master's degree for candidates.

Most candidates Ryman, Bell, Green and Michaels place in petrochemicals or polymers work in the plants, Miller says.

> We generally aren't looking for research people. If we were, we'd specify doctoral and postdoctoral candidates.
> Our clients want men and women with a minimum of three to five years' experience. They don't want trainees. They want people who can immediately jump in and do the job.

Qualified women and minority candidates are in demand. In this business, there's no such thing as discrimination for race or sex.

The initial placement process is fast. Miller says that within a week after Ryman, Bell, Green and Michaels receives a placement order, his firm can present at least five or six good candidates to the company. "With over 50 people, we work cooperatively," Miller says. "As many as 10 to 20 of us may work on a job order, in order to provide our clients with exceptional service."

Ryman, Bell, Green and Michaels places chemical and mechanical engineers, as well as chemists, into the polymer, petrochemical, and refinery industries. Patent attorneys are also in high demand and are recruited by the firm for these industries.

INTERVIEWS

If a client company is interested in a candidate, its department head or immediate potential superior sets up an appointment (through Ryman, Bell, Green and Michaels) for a phone conversation with the candidate. During the phone interview, Miller says, candidates generally receive background on the company. The company, in turn, uses the phone interview to learn the attitude and feelings of the candidate.

Next step, assuming all is proceeding smoothly: a face-to-face interview arranged by Ryman, Bell, Green and Michaels. "We set up everything, including plane tickets and hotel accommodations," Miller explains. "The candidate may be at the company one to four days, depending on how many people he or she has to see." Surprisingly, Miller almost never meets candidates he places; the process is handled almost entirely by telephone. "Oral and written communications skills are crucial for candidates," he says.

DO'S AND DON'TS

Miller believes resume-writing books and college placement officials don't talk much about the etiquette and courtesy required for candidates who deal with clients and an executive search firm.

"It's important that candidates keep us in the communications loop," he stresses. "Once we've arranged an interview on-site with a client company, we don't want to have to deal with our client to find out what went on. Candidates need to tell us what happened."

A "no" for candidates, Miller says, is discussing salary directly with the client. "If candidates attempt to negotiate money before a client decides whether the company wants to hire them, they're killed in the interview," he warns. "Allow the agency, as the facilitator, to do the negotiating—only after an offer is made."

Usually the client corporation's human resources department is *not* the decision-maker on hiring, Miller says. Most often, it's a "committee-type of decision," made by a group from the department in which the successful candidate will work.

The candidate may have a pretty good idea "from body language and attitude during on-site interviews" whether he or she has a chance at getting the job, Miller says. However, a serious offer is almost always made in writing—after the interview. Candidates usually have about 10 days to decide if they'll accept the offer. Miller says:

> That's the point when the client company and our firm decide what it takes to get this person. We do the negotiating, after the offer is made. Usually an organization is restricted on salary ranges and classifications. If candidates join the organization at midrange, there's room for four, five, or more years of salary growth within the range.

CHAPTER 7

KEEPING UP: SEMINARS, WORKSHOPS, CONVENTIONS

If your commitment to technical education stops when you pick up your first paycheck, you won't be employed very long. Because new materials and methods are continually being developed, the schooling you've received isn't enough to keep up.

As Dr. Roger Corneliussen, editor of *Drexel Polymer Notes,* puts it, "Opportunities are there for people—not so much in learning a specific skill for their jobs, but in developing their abilities to acquire knowledge."

SEMINARS AND WORKSHOPS

An excellent way to receive training in plastics technology is to enroll in the special industry seminars described in Chapter 3. These seminars, given at various locations around the country, are often sponsored by industry associations.

Training workshops and short courses are also presented by colleges and universities. Typical topics: Dispersion of Pigments and Resins in Fluid Media, and Applied Rheology for Industrial Chemists, both at Kent State University, Kent, Ohio; and Cross-linked Polymers: Chemistry, Properties, and Applications, and Polymers for Electronic Applications, each from the State University of New York at New Paltz. Technomic Publishing Company, Inc. has presented seminars on Advances in Medical Plastics, and Strategic Analysis Inc. has offered a conference on Profits in Recycling and Degradable Plastics.

CONVENTIONS

Another excellent strategy for growing professionally is to attend conventions and conferences. You'll be on the mailing list for information if you join any of the trade associations for plastics and related fields; most sponsor at least one conference a year.

Noteworthy in the plastics field are NPE, the National Plastics Exposition and Conference, held every three years and sponsored by the Society for the Plastics Industry, Inc. (SPI); ANTEC (annual trade show with over 30 technical seminars) and SPE Annual Plastics Recycling Fair, both sponsored by the Society of Plastics Engineers; Recyclingplas and Foodplas, sponsored annually by the Plastics Institute of America Inc.; and Pack Expo, which covers packaging machinery and materials.

Others include Polyurethanes, an annual conference sponsored by the Polyurethane Division of the SPI; EastPack '90: The Eastern Packaging Exposition, presented by Cahners Exposition Group; Composites in Manufacturing, a conference and exposition sponsored annually by the Society of Manufacturing Engineers (SME); AeroMat, a conference and exposition on advanced aerospace materials and processes, sponsored by ASM International; and SAMPE, an international symposium/exhibition sponsored by the Society for the Advancement of Material & Process Engineering. If you're interested in high-performance engineering thermoplastics and thermosets, check out the National Electronic Packaging and Production Conference (Nepcon West), which features those plastics in electronic applications. The 1990 show featured Dow Plastics' polycyanate resin for laminate/printed wiring board applications.

Don't forget, too, the annual meetings of societies like AIChE, the American Institute of Chemical Engineers, and SWE, the Society of Women Engineers. These organizations discuss many topics, including plastics, at their conventions, and you'll meet your counterpart members from various industries—a process which often leads to later networking.

A major reason for attending these conferences, if possible, is the technical knowledge and state-of-the-art information you'll pick up; a second reason is that many of them have a job fair—described as "a two-way employment-opportunities event."

Reading the trade publications will give you dates and locations for seminars, conferences, exhibitions, and workshops. Staying current on the meetings appropriate to your field is a way of continuing your professional growth.

CHAPTER 8

PLASTICS RESEARCH AND DEVELOPMENT

The plastics research and development professional is on the forefront of technology, discovering new polymers and composites and working to make a company's processes run more smoothly and efficiently. In 1980, according to a *Plastics World* survey, the average R&D professional had a bachelor's degree; by 1986, the magazine's survey showed he or she had a master's degree. And the trend, say the universities, is towards hiring those with new doctorates.

More than 85 percent of those surveyed in 1986 attended at least one trade show annually, and 23 percent attended three or four. Almost 75 percent of those researchers *Plastics World* surveyed in 1986 belonged to a professional society.

WHAT ANNUAL REPORTS SHOW

One way to learn how deeply a company is committed to R&D is to send for, and read from cover to cover, its annual report. Almost always, even in the corporations in which plastics, fibers, or composites are just a part of their overall business, you'll get a sense of what's going on and where the company hopes to go.

"Our chemical research effort continues to be focused on supporting our leadership position in certain specialty chemicals, as well as opening new markets for the future," says American Cyanamid Company. "Major projects are under way in . . . amino and isocyanate crosslinking resins, urethane chemicals, polymer additives for the industrial coatings market, adhesives and composites."

Chevron's R&D organization, Chevron Research and Technology Company, provides research and technical support to Chevron's downstream operating companies. Within the company, petrochemicals research concentrates on specialty polymers—chemicals that, because of their tolerance for high temperatures or impermeability to air and moisture, are used in high-tech plastic packaging.

While you may not find R&D budgets for plastics broken out as a line item in annual reports, you'll often see company-wide figures. For instance, overall Du Pont's R&D expenditures in 1990 totaled $1.44 billion, an increase of about 4 percent over 1989. Nearly 90 percent of these expenditures supported existing and developing businesses; the remaining 10 percent was spent by corporate labs on basic research to assure a strong long-range technological advantage for the company.

As part of Du Pont's R&D goal to move superior technology more rapidly from the lab to the marketplace, Du Pont has significantly strengthened its technical capabilities worldwide, especially in Europe and the Pacific Basin. In 1990, the company reported its technical staff outside the United States had increased by 20 percent from 1987–1989 to approximately 1,200 people, out of a worldwide total of 12,000 scientists, engineers, and technicians.

R&D AT DOW PLASTICS

Research and Development are important at Dow, a diversified worldwide manufacturer with 179 manufacturing sites in 31 countries, employer of 62,000 men and women around the world, and manufacturer of more than two thousand products. With the broadest range of thermoplastic and thermoset materials of any manufacturer, Dow ranks among the world leaders in the production of plastics. Dow plastics and plastic-fabricated products are used in a wide variety of applications in markets including packaging, automotive, electronics, appliances, building and construction, housewares, recreation, furniture, flooring, and health care.

Polymer performance and design/fabrication technology are helping plastics to be viewed as a preferred engineering material, Dow says—positioning which permits dramatic new solutions, often less expensive than metal, glass, or paper. With the global plastics industry growing at an estimated 4.5 percent annually, Dow's goal is to gain an increasing share of the global materials market through new applications and substitution of plastics for conventional materials.

Dave Beechuk, human resources manager for Dow Plastics' research and development laboratories, says the company looks for different kinds of people to perform its various job functions.

> When we're doing fundamental research, when we are looking at new molecules, new materials, and relationships of molecular structure to material properties, we will hire new Ph.D.'s who have specialized in material science, polymer science, and engineering. Their role is to help us develop and understand new materials, or to take existing technology and modify it to fit specifically identified needs. Or they may go off in totally new directions, developing new polymers that perform unlike anything else available.

Dow also hires polymer chemists with Ph.D.'s who help the company develop the processes for synthesizing those polymers. "They're doing basic research," Beechuk explains . . . "working out the chemistry, designing the chemical reactions required to produce the polymers."

Process Research

Process Research at Dow's R&D facilities is more short-range and directed than basic research, Beechuk says.

> The first group has identified a new polymer. Now it's the job of process research to make it economically. Most people here have been hired as new engineers, with B.S. or M.S. degrees. They consult with the Ph.D. chemical engineers, who have worked out the mathematical models of the process, developed the reaction kinetics, and, in general, dealt with the fundamentals of the chemical reactions taking place. The role of those in process research is to help the company economically, efficiently, and safely produce materials without harm to the environment.

Applications R&D

Another area within Dow Plastics' R&D organization includes men and women who work in applied product and applications research and development. These people are more externally focused, since their goal is to shape Dow technology to fulfill customer needs. "There's less emphasis on higher education—that is, the Ph.D. degree—requirements in this area," Beechuk says. "We usually hire at the B.S. or M.S. level. New Ph.D.'s tend to be more comfortable, and more closely matched, with a classical laboratory environment. Working in applications R&D

can also take you out of the lab and into the customer's plant.'' Beechuk explains:

> These application development personnel identify specific performance requirements that the polymer has when it's used by a customer, such as an automotive company. They then work with product development people to make our products suit the customer's needs. They also provide technical service to existing customers by helping them use Dow products effectively and safely.

Beechuk explains that such personnel are oriented towards specific markets: an automotive specialist, an electronics specialist, a packaging specialist.

> They anticipate our customers' needs. They also tend to be mechanically inclined—mechanical engineers, plastics engineers, and some chemical engineers—because they will develop the fabrication methods our customers use when they process the plastic materials.
>
> At this end of the spectrum, chemists play a much lesser role than engineers—except for working with those technologies that require us to develop specific formulations of Dow products with other materials . . . for instance, polymeric coatings.

HOW DOW PLASTICS RECRUITS

For those levels above applications development, Beechuk says, Dow recruits almost exclusively on campuses, doing almost all its hiring for these R&D positions from the pool of new graduates. "Once we start looking for people who are market-knowledgeable, however," he says, "we will also hire people with industrial experience. We look for people with the same skills our customers look for in their engineers; that is, if we want someone with knowledge of the automotive world, we would look for a person who would be attracted to work for a company like General Motors."

According to Beechuk, new hires with bachelor's or master's degrees start at salaries beginning in the low 30s to as high as the mid 40s. Specialized engineering degrees command the higher rates. Ph.D.'s can command a premium of $12,000–$20,000 per year over their counterparts with fewer degrees.

Lab assistants also are hired for research and development work at Dow. Generally, they have two-year degrees from pre-engineering programs. They're heavily oriented towards hands-on skills—data acquisition, fabrication know-how, ability to run equipment—but they have a math and science background sufficient to understand the fundamentals of what they are doing.

"They assist the professionals," Beechuk says. "Their duties vary—they may work in a chem lab at the front end, or out in the pilot plant, where they're making sample quantities of polymers. In the product and applications development area, they are making prototype parts for customers to test."

Starting salaries for lab assistants at Dow range from $20,000 to $25,000. For these positions, the company recruits nationally on junior college campuses.

Dow encourages continuing education at all levels, through tuition refunds and by promoting attendance at appropriate seminars, conferences, workshops, and conventions.

DOW LOCATIONS

Within the United States, Dow maintains plastics research and development facilities in Michigan, Texas, Louisiana, California, Georgia, and Ohio. Internationally, there are R&D labs in Canada

(Ontario), Switzerland, Spain, Germany, the Netherlands, Japan, Australia, Hong Kong, Brazil, Colombia, and Argentina.

"Although our people interact with each other globally," Beechuk says, "we have developed expertise in our technologies that's resident in all nations. We do not recruit on an international basis per se, since each geographical area is responsible for its own human resources."

CHAPTER 9

TECHNICAL SALES AND MARKETING

Plastics materials and resins are essentially not end products; instead, they are most often used to make other goods. Because of the advantages they offer, plastics and composites are becoming increasingly popular. The U.S. Department of Commerce calculates that the compound growth rate for the value of shipments of plastics materials and resins, between 1985 and 1988, was a whopping 17.0 percent. According to The Society of the Plastics Industry, Inc., which tracks industry facts and figures and publishes them annually, this places plastics far ahead of steel mill products (a compound growth rate of 5.3 percent), paper and board (8.8 percent), primary aluminum (3.7 percent), and synthetic rubber (1.0 percent).

As companies develop and introduce new plastics, and continue to produce successful resins, they face the problem of selling and marketing their products. Increasingly, in a competitive global market that targets more and more industries, sales and marketing personnel must have a technical background. They must be able to understand the products they are selling and help match customer needs with appropriate products.

If you enjoy sales and marketing, what chance do you have to be successful within the plastics industry? What background do you need? What training will you receive?

HIRING THE VETERANS

Janet Krikorian is manager of employment and employee relations for the plastics division of CIBA-GEIGY Corporation in Ardsley, New York. CIBA-GEIGY is a wholly owned subsidiary of CIBA-GEIGY Limited in Basel, Switzerland.

Krikorian recruits employees for the electronic materials, formulated systems, and resins groups of CIBA-GEIGY's plastics division, a major developer and producer of high-performance epoxy resins and hardeners. The products are used principally in marine and maintenance coatings, powder coatings, and civil engineering. According to Krikorian:

> We generally recruit for middle- to senior-level technical positions, including scientists, chemical engineers, chemists, and engineers. We look for candidates with undergraduate technical degrees and, for the senior-level positions, master's degrees and Ph.D.'s.
>
> We also recruit for technical sales and marketing positions. Potential candidates would hold a bachelor's degree in chemistry or chemical engineering, and have related industry experience.
>
> One of the entry-level positions we do recruit for is a technical sales associate. For this position, we might consider a CIBA-GEIGY employee who is currently working in the plastics division's lab and is interested in going into sales and marketing.

Employment agencies are a main recruiting source for CIBA-GEIGY's Plastics Division. According to Krikorian, agency selection is generally based on past placement history, quality of service, and location. Recruiting is done nationwide, but may be geared towards an area geographically close to where the candidate would be working.

THE HIRING PROCESS

The hiring process generally starts with Krikorian placing a job order with an agency, which then forwards resumes on possible candidates.

"I prefer to see resumes that list previous job experiences and dates," says Krikorian. "A resume that summarizes an applicant's life history without specific dates may indicate gaps in job history." According to Krikorian, CIBA-GEIGY looks for people with job stability—those who have three to four years' experience with a company.

After she has reviewed the resumes and matched them against the written job descriptions provided by the hiring manager, Krikorian works with the hiring manager to select several candidates. Potential candidates may be first interviewed over the phone by the hiring manager to screen interpersonal skills and to verify credentials listed on their resumes.

Once the candidates are selected, they are invited to a full-day interview with the hiring team. For technical positions, candidates are required to give a technical presentation to a group of as many as 10 to 15 people.

Interviews are usually conducted at the plastics division's headquarters in Ardsley, Hawthorne, or Tarrytown, New York. However, in situations where four or five candidates are from one area of the country, Krikorian and her hiring manager will occasionally travel there and be joined by the hiring manager handling the specific territory.

78   *Opportunities in Plastics Careers*

Following the interview, a decision may be reached on a particular candidate. However, a candidate may be called back a second time if further interviews with the division president or vice-president, for example, are necessary.

When a decision has been reached, the candidate is notified and asked for references. Krikorian explains:

> We call a minimum of two or three former employers or other appropriate sources. If all is favorable, we make a verbal offer, followed by a written confirmation.
>
> Following the written confirmation, a candidate is required to take a pre-employment physical and a drug test. We don't have random drug testing, but we do test every new employee. A new employee is officially hired after he or she successfully completes the pre-employment physical and drug test.

Newly hired sales people are brought into the plastics division's headquarters for one to three weeks' training. They tour the laboratories, meet people, and learn product lines. Following this period, they train with the marketing and sales people in their assigned territory. They may also spend time at a plant site where the products they will be selling are made. When it's time to enter the field, the sales manager or senior sales representative will orient and introduce the new employee to key customers.

PHILLIPS' PLASTICS PORTFOLIO

As manager of business development for the plastics division of Phillips 66 Company (a wholly owned subsidiary of Phillips Petroleum Company), Ray Ramsay has multiple responsibilities. Among them are the Plastics Technical Center, which provides a technical marketing service to the entire division; new products the company is developing; and sales, marketing, and product line training for the plastics division. This last duty is especially important because of different product lines in, as Ramsay calls it, "Phillips' portfolio of plastics."

Chemicals and plastics represent a $2.5 billion worldwide business for the company. Phillips has been in the plastics business over 35 years and has developed a products portfolio ranging from high-volume polyolefins, such as Marlex polyethylene and polypropylene, to a specialty transparent plastic called K-Resin, to a line of advanced materials like Ryton polyphenylene sulfide (PPS). Total volume is approaching three billion pounds per year.

Major Marlex polyethylene markets include blow molded containers, ranging from milk and bleach bottles to 55 gallon drums. Other markets include pipe for natural gas distribution and for municipal/industrial uses; film for merchandise bags, injection molded pails, and food containers; rotationally molded tanks for agricultural chemicals; and geomembranes for environmental applications such as pond liners. Marlex polypropylene is used to make bottle caps, housewares, food containers, straws, microwaveable containers, and many other injection molded or thermoformed products. Another major use is for fibers to produce a range of products from carpets, carpet backing, and upholstery to nonwoven fabric, strapping, rope, and geotextiles.

Phillips invented and manufactures K-Resin styrenebutadiene polymers, which combine transparency, impact resistance, and excellent processability. K-Resin polymers are used in many clear packaging applications, ranging from thermoformed clear cups to one-gallon bottles for drinking water. K-Resin polymers are also used to manufacture medical devices, toys, boxes, overcaps, and films.

High-performance engineering thermoplastics are a key part of the Phillips portfolio. Ryton polyphenylene sulfide (PPS) is used throughout the world in critical performance applications such as computer and telecommunications connectors. It's also used for harsh under-the-hood automotive applications because of its ability to withstand corrosive and high-temperature environments. Phillips AVTEL advanced composites use fiberglass and carbon fibers to produce high-performance products for commercial and military aviation as well as medical applications.

Recent developments in the Phillips portfolio include ASPECT TPPE and Crystalor PMP. The ASPECT TPPE is a thermoplastics polyester-based compound used in a variety of areas, including connectors, pump housings, and office furniture. ASPECT TPPE offers alternatives for the designers between Ryton PPS and Crystalor PMP in Phillips' continuum of products. Glass-reinforced Crystalor PMP is a midrange engineering resin belonging to the family comprising nylon, polycarbonate, PBT, polyacetal, and MPPO.

The thermal properties of Crystalor PMP make it the resin of choice for many under-the-hood applications, including reservoirs, end-tanks, and vacuum canisters. Crystalor PMP is also being developed for impact resistant applications, including bumpers and fascia. Crystalor also offers a unique combination of transparency, thermal resistance, chemical resistance release, and electrical insulation. These properties enable Crystalor PMP to address several markets including appliances, housewares, packaging, medical, and fibers.

THE RECRUITING PROCESS

Unlike some companies, Phillips prefers not to hire experienced people. "We want to recruit salespeople straight from college campuses," Ramsay explains, "and develop our own people."

The recruiting cycle begins nationwide in September for the next spring's graduates, he says. The company looks for chemical, mechanical, electrical, or plastics engineers, or those who have a technical degree in chemistry or physics. Salaries for those hired are competitive and vary by discipline. Phillips attempts to be in the top quartile of all financial offers made.

"We offer an excellent development position for potential management positions," Ramsay says. "That's why we're recruiting candidates for long-term growth with our company. We offer graduates a career versus a job."

Although grade point average (GPA) isn't the only criterion Phillips considers, Ramsay says it's significant because it reflects "raw horsepower. GPA often shows us the fundamental capacity of the individual," he explains. "When you find a person with a high GPA in a tough academic program, you'll usually find someone who's bright, disciplined, and self-starting. He or she has drive, and is willing to accept commitment."

Recruiters also look at candidates for qualities like resourcefulness and other signs of growth and achievement. Did they put themselves through school by working? What organizations were they involved with, and what roles did they play? How tough and durable are they? If they faced adversity, how did they recover? Do candidates seem seriously interested in long-term relationships? Also tops for Phillips: strong ethics.

> We can't consider anyone who gives us discomfort about their personal ethics. We're also concerned about fundamental interpersonal skills and how candidates will fit into the Phillips company culture. We're a southwestern United States corporation, headquartered in a small, family-type town. We're looking for people who can deal with peers and customers on a personal basis. We believe in a participative, team approach to working.

After initial screening, candidates for the sales, marketing, and technical training programs are brought to Phillips' headquarters in Bartlesville, Oklahoma, for several days, while sales managers from around the country fly in to interview them. Candidates also talk informally with Phillips' "rookies"—men and women who were hired the preceding year and are completing a year of intensive sales training. Ramsay says:

> Our recruiting system really works. Traditionally, in technical recruiting, you make two or three offers for every acceptance. However, of the offers we made following the final interview trip to Bartlesville in 1990, within two weeks we had a high level of confirmations and expect to have most all agree. These are really the top students. Some have dual degrees (an M.B.A. along with their engineering degree) or a master's in engineering. I feel certain that every person we invited here for interviews will get job offers from every company they've talked to.

TECHNICAL SALES AND MARKETING TRAINING

Within the plastics division, those who've been picked for technical sales and marketing positions begin a year of training at the Plastics Technical Center in Bartlesville. Training starts either in January or in July to coincide with the December and June graduating classes. Though they have standard working hours, most do a lot of outside-the-classroom studying, giving them effectively a 50-hour workweek.

"We call their main classroom the Rookie Room," Ramsay says. "There are computers and VCRs at workstations, but trainees can spin around from their desks and pull their chairs up to the conference table for discussion."

During initial training by veteran Phillips instructors, the rookies learn about the company and their plastics, and about competitors' plastics. Ramsay explains:

> They need to know all the things that will make them conversant and knowledgeable . . . characteristics of plas-

tics, and the plastics industry. They need to learn how our corporation operates and what its culture is. We teach them about corporate life and administrative things: how to fill out an expense report and what we mean by ethics. We role-play discussions between subordinates and supervisors.

In the second half of their training, rookies learn selling skills.

We move them out of Bartlesville to our various plants. They will visit Phillips Fibers Corporation in Greenville, South Carolina, and our pipe subsidiary, Phillips Driscopipe, headquartered in Dallas. They visit our major plastics manufacturing facility in Houston, and probably our Ryton PPS plant in the Texas Panhandle. They'll get hands-on opportunities in our labs, running processing machinery.

Rookies work the trade shows, helping to set up booths in San Francisco, Chicago, or Atlanta. It's suits-and-ties week, when they're in the hospitality suites or on the convention floor.

Until the last three months of training, rookies—by design—are generalists, with flexible assignments. Then matching begins, and rookies start to focus on particular products, learning them thoroughly. Rookies are also drilled in the systems they'll use as sales or territory managers.

When they've completed their formal training, rookies are sent into the field and begin to manage a sales territory. A "transition supervisor" takes them around, introduces them to customers, and helps them get acquainted with their territory before turning them loose. Ramsay explains:

Someone might be selling to General Motors. But they might be selling to three or four GM levels simultaneously. They may be calling on the people who write specs for corporate materials, but at the same time, they're seeing people at a body plant or motor plant—intermediate levels of manufacturing. They also could be calling on a plastics molder who is a vendor to General Motors.

In the electronics industry, they might be calling on AT&T, but, at the same time, talking to Bell Labs, meeting scientists who are doing fundamental work on plastics specs.

They might be calling on a manufacturer who makes disposable cups from our K-Resin. Although they could be meeting with the owner, they could also be down on the factory floor dealing with a shop foreman or supervisor to help work out a manufacturing problem.

The nice thing about our broad plastics business is that we get to participate in every business and industry in the United States. From aircraft to cars to appliances to food packaging, we get to participate as a partner with those companies. These days, our salespeople have to have broad knowledge about all the industries, but yet have a technical base so they can deal with the technical questions that are certain to come up. Many graduates of our training program are doing application development or product development work—helping our customers match our products to their needs, helping to create demand.

Moving Up

Within Phillips, Ramsay says, there are three ways that people can progress. From having a sales territory, they can move up the "typical management ladder," with several upgrades as a professional salesperson, to regional manager or supervisor. "You might become a special account-type representative," Ramsay says. Supervisors and managers can—and do—move from one product line to another. For instance, a recently appointed Ryton PPS manager has a background in polyethylene. Such a person might move to a marketing manager's position and end up as a vice-president.

A similar "senior professional ladder" (often chosen by people at the technical center) gives those who don't want to supervise or manage an opportunity for promotions and raises.

A third "technical ladder" is often elected by scientists at the technical center or those in R&D.

FUTURE OPPORTUNITIES

Ramsay sees opportunities in plastics growing—primarily because companies such as Phillips are upgrading the quality of living standards by improving the materials.

> In my father's time, plastics were often thought of as a cheap substitute. Today, in many applications, plastics are preferred because they do the job better than other materials.
>
> No industry in the United States could operate for ten minutes if its supply of plastics was shut off. You couldn't make a car; you can't make a television; you can't serve food. Plastics are totally integrated into our quality of life. Opportunities for a career in plastics are better now than they've ever been.

CHAPTER 10

MAKING ENGINEERING PLASTICS

More than ever before, producing engineering plastics has become a global industry. Although there are far more manufacturers of plastics products than there are resin or polymer producers, the economies of scale required for successful resin manufacturing demand large plants; that, of course, means many opportunities in plastics careers.

What are jobs in a plastics plant like? What's required to qualify? What do people holding these jobs *do*? A number of these questions are answered on the following pages by K. R. Davis, manager of human resources for the Hoechst Celanese plant in Bishop, Texas. Hoechst Celanese is the U.S. subsidiary of the German-based Hoechst Group. Their business lines include chemicals, fibers and films, and advanced materials, including engineering and high-performance plastics, paints and dyes, printing products, and pharmaceuticals.

ABOUT THE PLANT

The Bishop, Texas plant of Hoechst Celanese has been producing commercial chemicals for over 45 years. In 1961, the company brought on its first plastics line—for the production of acetal copolymers—and, in 1990, began manufacturing pharmaceutical products at the Bishop plant. "We use state-of-the-art technology," says K. R. Davis, human resources manager at the plant. "We've continued to upgrade our facility."

Bishop's employees (approximately 875) include those skilled in maintenance crafts—boilermakers, machinists, electricians, and electrical instrument technicians—and clerical/administrative support people. In addition, Davis says, the nonunion plant has lab technicians, chemical engineers, mechanical engineers, electrical engineers, chemists, chemical unit operators, and operator-helpers.

The Bishop plant is one of the company's largest producers of formaldehyde, with about 60 percent of this plant's formaldehyde output going into the production of acetal copolymer, one of the engineering plastics. Davis explains how the plastics are used:

> There's a lot of our product in General Motors automobiles and in kitchen appliances, like coffee pots, that require plastics with thermal properties around heating elements. Acetal copolymer is also used in plumbing products for the housing industry.
>
> A lot of the gears in large appliances are made from our plastics. We produce the plastic and ship it in pellet form to intermediate producers, who normally inject our product into molds, make the plastic parts, and ship them to manufacturers of consumer goods.

OPERATORS AND OPERATOR-HELPERS

The operator-helper position is an entry-level hourly position, Davis explains. "In our particular labor market, there aren't many people with prior experience in chemical processing. So we look for men and women with a high school education who have good work records, a willingness to work, and the ability to learn. We train them."

All new-hires go through one paid week of orientation, Davis says. They learn about Hoechst Celanese—the history of the plant, policies, and procedures. They're brought up-to-date with safety and environmental training.

Next, operator-helpers have three weeks of 40-hour-per-week paid training on the basics of distillation, heat transfer principles, basic principles of electricity, hand tools, instrumentation, and basic math that they'll use in gauging and ratios. "Gauging is taking a reading on the holding tank," Davis explains, "to learn how much material is in there. Do you have space, or do you need to close off the flow of product to the holding tank?" Also provided: training in reading blueprints and diagrams.

Once they've been assigned to a unit and started work as operator-helpers, trainees get an additional 12 weeks of instruction on the skills they need to do the various tasks associated with that unit. "The trioxine unit uses a different technology than the melt hydrolysis unit," Davis says. Trainees also learn safety information on chemicals and processes used in their assigned units.

Like all other production and laboratory jobs at the Bishop location, these positions are shift work. The facility is a seven-days-a-week, 365-days-a-year continuous processing plant.

"They'll work 7 A.M. to 3 P.M. for five straight days and then have two days off," Davis explains. "They then come back on a 3 P.M. to 11 P.M. shift for five days, followed by two days off. Next, they work 11 P.M. to 7 A.M. for five days, followed by four days off. To some extent, that presents a life-style challenge for them and their families."

Operator-helpers do some routine lab testing as well as gauging of certain tanks—opening and closing product transfer lines. They also have some duties connected with computer controls of the units. If an operator-helper is on the extruder line, he or she may keep the strands separated from each other as the strands go into the cooling bath, which hardens and sets the product. Operator-helpers make sure there's a smooth flow coming out of the extruder; they're usually the ones responsible for unplugging the line if it's stopped up, and they make sure the chopper works properly.

While someone's a helper, he or she is also learning how to become an operator, Davis says, which generally takes anywhere from two to five years of training. Overall good performance, good attendance, and a good safety record are qualities management considers in deciding on promotions. Both operator-helpers and operators receive a full range of benefits, and competitive pay.

Operators are primarily responsible for running the computer-controlled boards that operate the units, Davis says.

> They need to know how to bring up a unit and shut it down in an emergency. While the job isn't labor-intensive, we pay them for what they know and what they know how to do if the unit is not working properly. For instance, if the product is off-spec, they know what adjustments to make—when they can fix the problem themselves, and when they should call for help.

Operators are also eligible for promotion to shift supervisors, Davis says. Here, management looks for leadership qualities, problem-solving abilities, and the capability to facilitate team activities. First-line supervisors occasionally make a lateral move to become training coordinators/specialists.

OTHER PLANT EMPLOYEES

Also at Bishop: lab technicians, who do analytical testing of Hoechst Celanese's end-stream process and test finished products. Usually, they need about 12 hours of college chemistry to qualify for employment; Hoechst Celanese then trains them on individual analytical techniques. Because the plant runs round the clock, the technicians also are on rotating shifts. They can move up to be supervisors, and the supervisors, in turn, report to a group leader who is normally a chemist.

Although the plant uses warehouse people for packaging and shipping, Hoechst Celanese doesn't hire them. Instead, the company has contracted out those jobs—a deliberate management decision, Davis says, based on the fact that skills required for warehouse jobs didn't fit with the normal work progression for Hoechst Celanese employee development. Also, he says, if the industry should have an economic downturn, Hoechst Celanese wants the flexibility to reassign its own people.

RECRUITMENT AND HIRING

Hoechst Celanese's goal: "Every time we hire someone at the Bishop plant, we hope they'll spend their entire career with us," says Davis. "The plant's turnover rate is less than 1.5 percent per year for hourly employees, and less than 2.5 percent per year for all salaried employees. Consequently, when we hire, we really pay attention to the selection process."

Davis says the plant is the "preferred employer" of the community and has a 9-hole golf course and a swimming pool for employees and their families.

Recruitment isn't difficult, he says. For technicians, the company advertises in local papers within a 200-mile radius. Maintenance people, usually hired "from the outside," generally have five to seven years previous experience, not specialized in plastics, and they work as electricians, boilermakers, and machinists. When an operator-helper position opens, Davis says, within a week after the job is available, and without advertising, he may have 1,300 applications to screen. He says Hoechst Celanese probably interviews three persons for every one the plant hires.

Davis explains the company's hiring goals:

> We like to see people come in with a 'can do' attitude. We also look for men and women who are eager to work in a teamwork environment, who have a solid, stable work background, good human relations skills, and good communications skills.
>
> We use a team interviewing approach in which trained members of an interviewing team pose different questions to the applicants to give us examples of past performance in key dimensions appropriate for the job to be filled.

Davis says the company has identified six critical skills for each job; the team structures the interview by asking questions in which candidates reveal their abilities in these areas. "We ask applicants to give us a situation, describe the task, the activity required, and the results," he says. "We believe past performance predicts future behavior."

CHAPTER 11

OPPORTUNITIES IN A PLANT THAT USES PLASTICS

If you tallied up a scorecard of plastics manufacturers, you'd find about 300 U.S. plants making the resins that eventually become consumer products. Government figures, however, show there are far more plants—in virtually every state—that use plastics as a raw material, fabricating them into products that still may be intermediate, or into final finished goods. One such plant is Alpha Plastics, located in McHenry, Illinois, about fifty miles northwest of Chicago. Founder and owner John Meeson calls his factory unusual.

> You'd be hard-pressed to find anyone else who manufactures two thousand different items annually. Everything we do is a custom job, like the birth of a child. We've created so many of these products that we haven't even had time to put together flyers or a brochure telling what we do. Our customers don't care about sales literature. What they want is the least expensive cost-per-unit we can come up with.

CUSTOMIZED OPERATIONS

In Chapter 10, you read about Hoechst Celanese's Bishop, Texas plant—a continuous process plant that runs around the clock. Alpha Plastics is at the other end of the manufacturing spectrum; it's a job shop deliberately designed to change, retool, and adapt machines and workers to produce short runs of many individual products. The company's custom-produced items are sold across the United States and, to a limited extent, in European markets.

Meeson says his 25 years of industry experience have given him the ability to schedule, plan, meet customer deadlines, and customize his plant operations "faster and quicker than any software program ever written, or than a mainframe computer." A former Wisconsin farm boy, Meeson had other ambitions than a stay-on-the-farm future. As he puts it, "I got tired of shoveling gutters out, baling hay, and working a back-busting 14 hours a day bringing in the crops." He earned a marketing degree from DePaul University and a master's in business administration from Northwestern University. The technical side? "I taught myself," he says.

Alpha Plastics specializes in creating heat-sealed vinyl products in many different forms, shapes, and styles. Meeson says:

> When individuals in the marketplace are looking for someone to manufacture a product, they call the plastics mills and the equipment manufacturers. They say, "We want a widget that will fly, and it will be decorated in 17 colors and will dive underwater." And they're told, "Call Alpha Plastics because they are the company that can transfer all your dreams into a finished product."

The company's output includes disposable medical products, computer software packaging, briefcases, binders, PocketSavers, inflatable cushions, and advertising specialty giveaway items. "If you walk into Sears or Ace Hardware," Meeson says, "you'll see twist drills, socket sets, and ratchet wrenches, all in *our* heat-sealed vinyl packaging. We produce items for probably 25 different industries—things you'd never imagine. For instance, if you look at a barber chair, you'll see it's tufted, channeled, and embossed. We do that embossing.''

ON THE FACTORY FLOOR

Supervisor Marge Kuhns, who has been with Meeson for over 10 years, began as an operator and still trains new employees on each machine. Currently, Alpha Plastics has 30 employees on the factory floor; that number can go temporarily to 50 or 75, depending on particular job orders. If work is slow, Kuhns says, Meeson may ask an employee to take one day a week off—but hasn't laid anyone off in the last ten years, she says.

New-hires earn $4 to $4.25 an hour—more, as they learn. A set-up operator, who has the know-how and training to adjust the machines' gauges and temperatures as required for a particular job order, is paid more. Work starts at 7 A.M. and is usually completed by 3 P.M. Employees get 30 minutes for lunch and two 10-minute coffee breaks. Although employees don't receive health benefits, they are eligible for profit sharing.

Plastics come into the plant on rolls, are slit to the correct size for the particular product Alpha's making, and are put on the press. The die under the press is changed for different jobs.

Some workers are on machines that require them to move the plastic back and forth by hand; others are on machines with turntables that automatically rotate to bring fresh materials or take product away. One such machine, with two workers, has a nearby robot, programmed to pick up the material and lay it at the same spot every time. ''The robot's efficient,'' says Kuhns, ''and it eliminates the need for one person.''

Meeson, the owner of the business, believes in robotics, but he has some reservations:

> In a small business like mine, you can't just plunk down a couple hundred thousand dollars on a robot that's going to run a job for a week or so. The trick is to be able to develop robotic systems inexpensively that are adaptable across the wide number of operations. Since robotic technology is in its infancy, most engineers and technicians can develop a robot easily for a specific application—but to have a multi-use robotic environment is extremely difficult. We need a robot that, after it performs its function, we can move it over to Table B, and it begins a new function. When Table B is finished, we want to move the robot to Table C to work.

Among the company's most popular products: bags with zippers, bags printed with a customer's logo, manicure sets (which combine a sealed-on pocket with a form board), silk-screened products with colors and designs, binders, and heat-sealed vinyl plastic packaging for art supplies, markers, and pens.

Kuhns sees her supervisor's role as a combination of teaching ("I show them the most efficient way to work") and mothering. "If they have a little problem at home, or they're feeling blue, I try to help them feel better," she says. She tries to switch employees around to different machines so they don't become tired and bored on a job. "If you always work the same job every day," she says, "you begin to get careless." A major benefit of switching: "Everyone is trained for every job, so if someone's absent, we can put a person on that machine right away."

WORKERS' QUALIFICATIONS

Finding dependable workers isn't easy for Alpha Plastics, or for many other manufacturing firms. Meeson describes the work as "menial and mundane" and says those with too much potential get bored too quickly. "Labor is a difficult resource," he says. "Society has changed, and America is no longer a manufacturing nation; more people are in service industries, and we've forgotten how to make things. We need people who want to work hard—and they're difficult to find."

Kuhns says a high school diploma isn't required as a condition of employment, but new-hires have to be able to read and write in English. Ability counts; some jobs are more technical than others and require higher skills.

Initiative and resourcefulness are pluses, she says. "In this kind of a plant, the people really work on their own," she explains. "They have to inspect their own work. They need to catch anything wrong—either to fix it themselves by adjusting a machine or to call someone to repair it. They must be conscientious about the product they're making." Another "must"—the ability to work well with other people, since the machines are adjacent.

Kuhns also values the ability to be trained and to be organized, since helter-skelter work is not efficient. Kuhns does feel that someone who wants to get ahead needs college courses, especially in math and "people skills," in order to be able to organize people so they understand what they have to do.

FUTURE OPPORTUNITIES

Though he's still spending most nights and parts of every weekend at Alpha Plastics, Meeson wouldn't change. "After 25 years I still feel I'm in the right field," he says. "I can't wait to get out of bed and go to work!" Meeson sees plastics as offering a great future.

"There's no question about it," Meeson says. "The natural resources on our planet are getting used up. Consequently, we have to come up with synthetic materials. Once iron ore disappears, thermoplastics are going to be the basic raw material element for our planet. That means lots of opportunity.''

CHAPTER 12

OPPORTUNITIES IN PLASTICS RECYCLING

Late in 1990, three events occurred which will affect your opportunities for careers in plastics recycling.
1. McDonald's, the world's largest quick-service restaurant organization, with more than 11,400 restaurants in 53 countries, announced its intent to phase out foam packaging.
2. The Coca-Cola Company and Hoechst Celanese Corporation together announced plans to introduce plastic soft drink bottles made with a blend of recycled plastic, a significant breakthrough in plastics recycling.
3. Pepsi-Cola Company and The Goodyear Tire and Rubber Company together announced their plans to introduce soft drink beverage bottles containing recycled polyethylene terephthalate (PET)—the first time recycled plastic packaging will be used in direct contact with food.

To understand how these developments in plastics recycling can affect your possible career in the field, you need to know something of the background behind them, and of the challenges (both technical and economic) which plastics recycling faces in the next decade.

ENVIRONMENTAL ISSUES

A major 1990 industry study, "Issues and Trends in the Plastics and Rubber Industries," was conducted by the Gary Siegel Organization for Berger, Goldstein Capital Group, Inc. The study focused on the perceptions of executives in the plastics and rubber industries on current business trends and practices, and on timely issues affecting their industry.

As the study's executive summary concludes, "environmental issues will be the flash point of the 1990s in the plastics industry." Plastics industry executives in nine midwestern states cite solid waste disposal and biodegradable products as major environmental issues.

These environmental issues are growing in importance, the study found. In fact, the executives surveyed—two-thirds of whom were presidents, chief executive officers (CEOs), or chief operating officers (COOs) of their companies—mentioned the importance of environmental issues just as often as they mentioned cost or financial factors. Seventeen percent of the executives who responded believed that over the next two to three years environmental issues would have the greatest impact on how products are manufactured. More respondents chose environmental issues than "financial," "foreign competition," "government," or "labor/work force" as the major factor influencing manufacturing. The executives believed that in the coming years the effect of cost factors on manufacturing will be overshadowed by environmental issues.

Perceptions Influence Actions

What's behind some of the environmental issues that have plastics executives worried? Often, it's consumer *perceptions*—beliefs many of us hold. Our perceptions can influence a corporation's actions.

For instance, McDonald's launched a large polystyrene recycling program in October, 1989. Polystyrene, used in a number of industries, is perhaps most familiar as foam packaging. The recycling program began with 450 McDonald's restaurants in the New England area, and it spread throughout McDonald's 8,500 U.S. locations. Customers of those restaurants separated their polystyrene and other plastic packaging into separate trash bins. The separated polystyrene went to a plastic recycler to be made into items such as videocassette casings, home insulation board, and even McDonald's own restaurant trays.

As McDonald's pointed out in its spring 1990 flyers, polystyrene foam packaging is recyclable. It's over 90 percent air; it compresses easily under pressure, and it breaks apart cleanly in landfills. Because it does not biodegrade, it's considered nontoxic in landfills.

But in late 1990, McDonald's announced its intent to phase out foam packaging, starting in spring, 1991. Ed Rensi, president of McDonald's USA, said the phaseout would start with foam sandwich containers, which account for nearly 75 percent of McDonald's total foam use.

"Although some scientific studies indicate that foam packaging is environmentally sound, our customers just don't feel good about it. So we're changing," said Rensi. "We've been testing packaging options, and we're confident we have found some good alternatives that address our customers' concerns while maintaining our strict quality standards." An important environmental benefit of this change is a significant reduction in the volume of packaging used by McDonald's.

Rensi said the move was part of a comprehensive environmental initiative being developed by McDonald's and the Environmental Defense Fund (EDF). The two groups had been working together for several months before the announcement. Fred Krupp, executive director of EDF, said, "McDonald's has scored an environmental touchdown, and through our continuing joint efforts with the task force, we're expecting more good news in the future. This action is the beginning of a new era of environmental problem solving.''

Jim Cantalupo, president of McDonald's International, explained:

> The company will continue to test for the best alternatives for the remaining packaging, and will phase them into our restaurants as they become available.
>
> At the same time, we'll be continuing our commitment to recycling, our use of recycled materials, other source reduction initiatives, and additional environmental projects. These changes are not expected to affect prices to our customers or restaurant profitability.

Many plastics executives saw the McDonald's announcement as a reaction to consumer pressure. In response, Ron Evason, president of The Society of the Plastics Industry of Canada (SPI), said that ''the public's elated reaction to McDonald's Restaurants' decision to phase out the use of polystyrene clamshells only serves to highlight and perpetuate the all-too-common myths and misconceptions about polystyrene.''

MYTHS ABOUT PLASTICS

What do you believe about plastics and their contribution to municipal solid waste? Do you agree or disagree with the following statements?

- Plastics are a major cause of the solid waste problem.
- Switching to traditional materials or ''degradable'' materials for packaging will substantially help the problem.
- Massive recycling will solve the solid waste problem.

- Plastics cannot be recycled because plastics recycling is not cost-effective.
- Recycling has to be profitable as a stand-alone venture.

Chances are that you—and certainly many people—believe that at least some of the statements just given are true. Yet *all* are myths, according to Dr. Sidney Rankin of the Center of Plastics Recycling Research at Rutgers, the State University of New Jersey.

The truth is that plastic beverage containers have the second highest "scrap value" of recyclable materials in packaging—next to aluminum. In fact, more than 20 percent of all plastic soft drink containers—over 100 million pounds—are already being recycled into new consumer products, and the demand for recycled plastic is growing. In 1987, 55 million pounds of the plastic used in milk containers were recycled.

Just how big is the plastics waste problem? What do consumers believe, and how accurate are their beliefs?

In the United States, we generate over 180 million tons of municipal solid waste each year—more than one-half ton per person. And the amount is rising steadily at the rate of slightly over one percent per year. The Environmental Protection Agency estimates that each person in the United States generated 3.6 pounds of garbage per day in 1986; by 2000, daily per-person garbage is expected to increase to 3.9 pounds.

How much of that waste do plastics represent? The answer is determined, in part, by how you're counting. In 1988, by weight, plastics contributed only 8 percent to that total, but by volume, they represented about 20 percent of municipal solid waste. Yard and food waste, by comparison, account for 29 percent of the solid waste stream, while paper and paperboard account for 35 percent.

Partially because of the growing volume of disposable packaging, the resulting high profile for plastics, says the Plastics Institute of America, has made plastics in all forms the target of environmentalists and legislators everywhere. As plastics in a variety of applications are being banned by federal, state, and local authorities, whole markets are threatened—and so are jobs. While there are ways to dispose of plastics and products made from them, the options are dwindling. Six thousand landfills currently in use account for about 80 percent of all municipal trash in the United States, but one-third of these are expected to close by 1994. Incineration, which burns another 10 percent of total municipal trash, has many environmentalists fuming over what they consider potential harmful emissions. One seemingly attractive option—making plastics biodegradable—has drawbacks. It's easier said than done; it negates the positive impact of recycling programs, and no one is yet sure whether degradables may actually aggravate existing problems. In fact, says the Office of Technology Assessment (OTA), it's still unclear whether "degradables" actually degrade into environmentally safe by-products.

Recycling is an option many consumers may support in theory, but few are presently following. Experts believe about 10 percent of total municipal trash is currently being recycled—most of it, paper.

As for the rest of municipal solid waste, other products are being recycled. Glass (0.7 percent), aluminum (0.4 percent), and steel (0.2 percent) outrank plastics, according to data from Franklin Associates. OTA says that in 1986, less than 100,000 tons of post-consumer plastic discards—which represented less than one percent of the amount in municipal solid waste—were recycled. While plastic recycling from municipal solid waste rose to 200,000 tons in 1989, it is clear there's a long way to go.

"Some people who see this data wonder why plastics don't have a better track record for recycling," says Wayne Pearson, executive director of the Plastics Recycling Foundation.

However, we need to remember that we've been recycling glass, aluminum, steel, and paper for 50 years—long before plastics came into widespread use. People are used to recycling those other materials.

Plastics recycling percentages are small because plastics recycling got a late start. But in the first ten years since the plastic beverage container was introduced, it's had a recycling record of 28 percent. That's a recycling rate curve as steep, or even steeper, than aluminum cans.

PLASTICS RECYCLING FOUNDATION

Plastics offer many advantages in packaging. They've become increasingly popular, replacing other products. Plastic packaging is versatile, protective, and convenient to use, shape, and manufacture. In fact, plastic products provide safety and health benefits for which no other material is equally suited—including tamper-evident foods and medicines, shatter-resistant containers, freezer-to-microwave prepared foods, and wrappers that preserve freshness.

The 15 billion pounds of plastic packaging produced each year currently account for about 13 percent of all packaging. And, though plastic packaging only amounts to about 4 percent (by weight) of all municipal solid waste, its share of that waste is increasing.

Eliminating plastics in packaging, however, isn't necessarily the answer to trash problems. A 1987 West German study that examined ecological and economic consequences from such a move estimated that replacing plastic with other materials would increase packaging weight four times, increase packaging volume 2.5 times, and double the energy required for production.

In 1985, concerned members of the plastics packaging industry established the Plastics Recycling Foundation, an independent, not-for-profit, nonpolitical foundation seeking solutions to recycling questions through a partnership of business, government, and education. The foundation's mission is to validate through research that recycling plastic packaging is a business that is technically and economically feasible, and environmentally beneficial.

The foundation established the Center for Plastics-Recycling Research at Rutgers–The State University of New Jersey to conduct this research. Other universities involved include New Jersey Institute of Technology, Michigan State University, the University of Toledo, Case–Western Reserve, and Rensselaer Polytechnical Institute. Additional funding is being provided by the New Jersey Commission on Science and Technology, the Council for Solid Waste Solutions, the National Science Foundation, and the states of Ohio, Michigan, and New York.

WHAT IT TAKES TO RECYCLE PLASTICS

Experts believe there are four criteria for successful recycling:
1. A continuous source of scrap
2. Viable technology for recycling
3. End-use applications and markets for products derived from the wastes
4. Good economics

Wayne Pearson, executive director of the Plastics Recycling Foundation, looks at the economic issues and how they affect future jobs in plastics recycling.

"First, the recyclable material must be collected," he says. "Next, the material must be sorted by generic type, if the collection system involves mixed products. Then the quality of the recovered material must be enhanced through reclamation. And finally, the recycled material must be sold into end-use markets.''

In communities with recycling programs, typically a collection truck picks up the recyclables. In some towns, consumers have done initial sorting—keeping plastic containers such as milk jugs and beverage bottles separate from newspapers, glass, and aluminum cans. In other towns, trucks take all recyclables to a municipal sorting facility, or MRF.

A major problem in recycling is that in a user's mind, plastics are interchangeable and often look alike. In a curbside program that asks users for only soda beverage bottles and gallon milk jugs, typically 15 to 30 percent of what the collection truck picks up includes other types of plastic bottles, some of which are multi-layered or pigmented.

Yet plastics disposables need to be separated by type in order to have the most value for a buyer who wants to use recycled plastic. If you're a manufacturer who uses polyethylene terephthalate, known as PET, you don't want to have to buy a bale of recycled materials containing a mixture of other plastics such as polyvinyl chloride (PVC) because it costs money to remove the contaminants. You won't pay a premium price for a combination of plastics. Instead, you'll use virgin resin instead of recycled products because your process needs the ''pure'' material.

Separating the various types of plastic is crucial to successful recycling. During the reclamation process, even a small amount of PVC in a batch of as many as 6,000 PET bottles interferes with the recovery of the PET. In addition, PVC in the PET stream can damage molding machinery by generating hydrochloric acid.

Wayne Pearson explains the importance of sorting:

> To make recycling economically viable, you've got to sort effectively. At Rutgers University, in the Center for Plastics Recycling, we're working on ways to make the sorting technology practical. Some of our techniques are derived

from ore-mining technology. Another technology that lets plastic bottles be scanned on an automatic sorting line is an adaptation of an X-ray detector. The instrument is so sensitive that a PVC label on a PET bottle will trigger the detector, so that the bottle can be removed from the line. These automatic sorting lines also use photocells to identify and separate clear, green, natural, and opaque plastic bottles. Currently, the automatic technology permits detection of 600 bottles a minute.

Technically all plastics are relatively easy to recycle. And since plastics are derived from petroleum, if oil prices rise, Pearson believes it will be cheaper for manufacturers to use recycled plastics than to produce virgin resins.

A Technology Breakthrough

One barrier to the use of recycled plastics for certain applications has been the U.S. Food and Drug Administration, which traditionally has not permitted products made with recycled resins to be used in direct contact with food in packaging. That prohibition, however, may soon be modified.

By weight, consumer soft drink packaging represented only 1.6 percent of the total solid waste stream in 1990. The industry has been conscious, however, of the need to scale down packaging and reduce sources of weight. For instance, since 1984, Pepsi-Cola Company has reduced the amount of material used in plastic, aluminum, and glass by 28 percent, 35 percent, and 25 percent, respectively. Since 1970, more than 210 billion soft drink containers (aluminum, steel, glass, and plastic) have been recycled by the soft drink industry. Among them: beverage bottles containing PET, recycled at a 28 percent rate.

Until now, the more than 200 million pounds of plastic soft drink containers recycled in the United States have been used in making carpeting, fiberfill stuffing for jackets and comforters, lumber, piping, patio furniture, and nonfood bottles. But a breakthrough technology announced almost simultaneously in December, 1990, by The Coca-Cola Company and Pepsi-Cola Company, along with their resin suppliers, has expanded the end-use markets for recycled plastic containers.

The Coca-Cola Company, headquartered in Atlanta, Georgia, is the world's largest producer of syrups and concentrates for carbonated beverages. The company's products lead all major segments of the $43 billion domestic soft drink industry, accounting for more than 41 percent of all soft drinks sold.

Commercially viable technology, developed by The Coca-Cola Company and Hoechst Celanese Corporation, breaks down plastic soft drink bottle polymer into original molecules, then reconstructs the purified resin for use in making new plastic soft drink bottles.

"Producing new plastic beverage bottles with a blend of recycled plastic is a significant step ahead in plastics recycling," says M. Douglas Ivester, senior vice-president of the Coca-Cola Company and president of Coca-Cola USA. "The technology will allow the 'closed loop' recycling of our plastic bottles, just as our other suppliers use recycled aluminum and steel for cans and recycled glass for glass bottles."

In a similar press release, Pepsi-Cola Company announced what it termed "an environmental breakthrough—the use of recycled plastic in Pepsi's soft drink bottles." While Pepsi's current polyethylene terephthalate (PET) bottles are recyclable into end uses like carpet fiber and park benches, Pepsi spokesman Andrew Giangola explained, a new breakthrough manufacturing process allows PET materials to be reused safely again and again in beverage containers, thus "closing the loop" on plastics recycling.

"The soft drink industry has long been an innovator in packaging and a leader in recycling," says Craig Weatherup, president and chief executive officer of Pepsi-Cola Company.

Pepsi's first recycled PET bottles are being manufactured by Sewell Plastics, Inc. of Atlanta, Georgia, using Repete, a trademarked recycled resin produced by The Goodyear Tire and Rubber Company of Akron, Ohio. Goodyear spent two years developing Repete. The recycled resin is created by grinding used soft drink containers which are depolymerized, a process that breaks down the original material's building blocks. Then the PET flake is repolymerized—or put back together—and combined with virgin raw materials to meet strict safety standards for food containers.

"Basically, Repete takes PET bottles back to components that can be purified," says Jim Stanley, Vice-President, Scientific and Regulatory Affairs, Pepsi-Cola Co. "Bottles made with Repete will be no different in quality and safety than bottles made entirely with virgin materials."

After the FDA has reviewed and okayed the recycled product for food contact use, plastic bottles with a total recycled PET content of approximately 25 percent will be scheduled for introduction—first, in the northeastern United States and then throughout Pepsi's U.S. distribution channels.

PLASTICS RECYCLING JOBS

What kinds of opportunities are open if you'd like a career in plastics recycling? No one has all the answers, since the field is changing rapidly.

"There are a number of career possibilities," says Jose Fernandes, a project manager at the Center for Plastic Recycling Research. Fernandes is a mechanical and industrial engineer with a background in packaging engineering. He had several years' experience in the packaging industry before joining the center's staff when it opened in 1985. Fernandes believes the recycling industry offers many opportunities.

> I believe the recycling industry will continue to grow steadily. In the technical areas, you'll need engineers to develop new methods and equipment that make recycling more economical and technically easier. At a recycling plant, you'll find managers, maintenance engineers, and mechanics, foremen and welders . . . similar jobs to those you'd find in any industrial facility.
>
> One approach to plastics recycling is to design packages specifically to make recycling easier . . . for that, a background in packaging or materials or polymer science is helpful.
>
> And on the human side, you'll find people who work in urban studies. You see, collecting recyclable items isn't that simple. Communities vary. You'll find different quantities and types of items, depending on whether you're picking up from single-family households of multidwellings . . . depending on the particular culture and public attitudes. For instance, McDonald's move to phase out styrofoam packaging in response to public pressure will change the composition of what's picked up from their restaurants.
>
> There'll be a need for people to do these kinds of studies, as well as a need for those experienced in economics, management, and even statistics.

Dr. Tom Nosker, another project manager at the center, sees additional opportunities in product development.

> In general, the polymer chemists have not yet investigated what can be done when you mix commodity plastics together.
>
> Suppose, for instance, you had a recycled resin in which you had two different kinds of plastics: one glassy, one

rubbery. If you could process this hypothetical mixture in such a way that the glassy fibers could be aligned in the direction of applied stress, you'd have a potentially valuable new product.

We'll need people who can work with those sorts of ideas . . . who have imagination and technical training . . . who can develop processing techniques to make these potential products.

We'll need engineers to develop better equipment for automated sorting and materials handling. Right now, we can identify and sort some of the different kinds of plastics. But how do you move empty plastic bottles, which are light in weight, down a belt to go past metal detectors, without having them fly off?

We'll need better collection systems that are more sophisticated in handling various sizes and types of items. Someone will have to design them and test them. That person could very well be you.

I predict a large number of new recycling-related jobs over the next five to ten years. That's because there are powerful driving forces behind recycling. Society needs an alternative way of disposing of waste. Society also needs to conserve the resources in our trash.

Consequently, the recycling industry will be working hard to increase the rate of recycling as quickly as it's economically possible.

Already, we've worked out many of the recycling technologies. As soon as the business and public sectors believe it makes economic sense to invest the necessary capital, job opportunities in recycling will grow rapidly.

RECYCLING ORGANIZATIONS

Listed below are a number of nonprofit organizations that are active in supporting plastics recycling programs and technology

112   *Opportunities in Plastics Careers*

research. You can contact any of them for further information on plastics recycling programs. They are taken from *1989 Recycling Directory,* published by Society of the Plastics Industry, Inc.

Center for Plastics Recycling Research
  Rutgers University
  Building 3529, Busch Campus
  Piscataway, NJ 08855

Provides: technical/statistical information; conducts and supports research on the recycling of post-consumer plastic waste.

Society of the Plastics Industry, Inc.
Council for Solid Waste Solutions
  1275 K Street, NW
  Suite 400
  Washington, DC 20005

Provides: literature and information on recycling and other solid waste management options for plastics.

Council on Plastics and Packaging in the Environment
  1275 K Street, NW
  Suite 900
  Washington, DC 20005

Provides: forum for discussion, literature, and information on solid waste management issues concerning plastics and packaging.

Keep America Beautiful
  9W Broad Street
  Stamford, CT 06902

Provides: recycling educational guidance based on a national network of community recycling programs.

National Association for Plastic Container Recovery
  5024 Parkway Plaza Boulevard
  Suite 200
  Charlotte, NC 28217

Provides: information on establishing comprehensive community and state recycling programs, based on facilitation and education efforts nationwide. Information on recycling of PET bottles.

The Plastic Bottle Information Bureau
1275 K Street, NW
Suite 400
Washington, DC 20005

Provides: information on plastic bottle issues related to solid waste and recycling to various audiences; makes available copies of its directory, the Plastic Container Code System, *Recycling Today,* the PBIB literature list, and other publications.

Plastics Recycling Foundation
P.O. Box 189
Kennett Square, PA 19348

Provides: information and literature on the Plastics Recycling Foundation and recycling research it sponsors.

Polystyrene Packaging Council
1025 Connecticut Avenue, NW
Suite 513
Washington, DC 20036

Provides: information on legislative activity and industry initiatives concerning the recycling of polystyrene foam materials.

The Vinyl Institute
155 Route 46 W
Wayne, NJ 07470

Provides: literature and information concerning recycling and potential markets for recycled PVC.

Many other groups, such as those listed below, support plastics recycling on the state, regional, or municipal level. For information on plastics recycling in your area, contact your state legislator or your mayor's office.

Plastic Recycling Corp. of California
3345 Wilshire Boulevard
Suite 1105
Los Angeles, CA 90010

Provides: educational information on plastics recycling in California, including technical, promotional, and financial assistance, to communities with curbside programs.

Plastic Recycling Corp. of New Jersey
P.O. Box 6316
North Brunswick, NJ 08902

Provides: various forms of marketing, technical, capital, and public education assistance to counties, municipalities, and private organizations engaged in recycling in New Jersey.

CHAPTER 13

WOMEN AND MINORITIES

There's good news and bad news about opportunities for women and minorities who want careers in plastics technology. The good news is that sex and ethnic origin are no barriers to qualified candidates. In other words, if you have the prerequisite skills and desire, you have excellent chances of finding employment; in fact, say some of the executive search firms, you'll be in demand. Companies within the industry, while not necessarily giving special preference to women and minorities, often are interested in increasing their recruitment of qualified candidates. In fact, a number of companies actively participate in consortia deliberately designed to encourage minority enrollment and success in engineering and related fields. The bad news is that proportionately fewer women, blacks, and Hispanics are studying engineering. In short, the pool of qualified women and minority job applicants is being reduced.

CONCENTRATE ON SCIENCE AND MATH

If you are a woman or a member of a minority group, what can you do to become qualified to work in plastics technology? One important strategy is to excel in science and mathematics. As a junior high or high school student, sign up for all the math and science possible. Often, especially in large metropolitan areas such as Chicago or Atlanta, there are opportunities for enrichment programs in those subjects. Even if such programs require your after-school, weekend, or vacation time, take advantage of everything you can. The skills you gain and the contacts you make can be invaluable. Also, as you begin to read about schools with courses and degrees in polymer science; chemical, packaging, or materials science engineering; or chemistry; write to the director of admissions at those institutions that interest you. Ask about summer studies, minority recruitment, or special programs you can join.

One reason for picking up additional math and science beyond that taught in your regular high school's curriculum is that there are serious shortages of qualified high school teachers. One survey by the National Science Teachers Association concluded that almost one-third of all high school students are being taught science or math by teachers who are not qualified. In addition, a survey of State Title II directors showed that over 200,000 math teachers and 319,000 science teachers need further in-service training. Half the high school science teachers, the survey discovered, have had less than six hours of in-service training in science within the past year.

A January, 1989, international assessment of mathematics and of science carried out by the Educational Testing Service reported that students in the United States ranked in or near the lowest grouping among 13-year-olds tested. The results of proficiency testing in performing mathematical computations, similar to results reported in science proficiency, ranked United States students behind Korea, Quebec (French), British Columbia, Quebec (English), New Brunswick (English), Ontario (English), New Brunswick (French), Spain, United Kingdom, Ireland, and Ontario (French). Statistics from the National Research Council indicate that the mathematics achievement of the top five percent of the 12th grade students is lower in the United States than in other industrialized nations. The average 12th grade mathematics student in Japan outperforms 95 percent of comparable U.S. 12th graders.

Early Choices

New research about career choices has brought to light some disturbing facts. Based on a Rockefeller Foundation study by Sue E. Berryman entitled "Who Will Do Science?," the Committee on the Status of Women in Physics made this report:

> [By ninth grade], over one-third of those who will earn a quantitative bachelor's degree already expect to pursue a career in science. By the end of twelfth grade, the pool is fully established. A necessary component of the pool's educational profile is the completion of advanced high school math. This optional sequence, which is elected by one-third fewer girls than boys, marks the first point at which the educational profiles of the two sexes diverge.

Young women, then, are skipping courses that could lead them to lucrative and challenging science careers—in plastics technology, as well as in other scientific fields. In particular, such women are turning off early on the math they need to succeed.

Two Critical Decision Points for Women

Even though physics would not seem to be the science of choice if you're looking for a career in plastics technology, students in all branches of engineering need a thorough grounding in physics.

The Committee on the Status of Women in Physics (CSWP) publishes a quarterly newsletter. It has reported two major decision points for women: points where choices must be made about future educational investment.

The first point comes much earlier than most students realize. By ninth grade, over one-third of those who will later earn a bachelor's degree in quantitative fields (math, physical or biological sciences, computer science, engineering, or economics) already expect to be scientists. By the end of twelfth grade, the pool is fully established; that is, essentially all those who will go on to a bachelor's degree in quantitative science have already decided to do so.

To succeed in any of these technical fields, you need a strong math background. Yet advanced high school math is elected by one-third fewer females than males. Of those who completed the necessary high school math sequence, according to the Scientific Manpower Commission, only 21 percent of the young women, as compared to 51 percent of the young men, chose a quantitative field when declaring their undergraduate majors.

"These two turning points account for more than two-thirds of the extra loss of women compared to their male peers all the way through the Ph.D. degree," says the CSWP *Gazette*.

SOCIETY OF WOMEN ENGINEERS

A major organization that tracks the achievements and statistics of women in engineering is the Society of Women Engineers (SWE). It offers pamphlets and information on scholarship programs, convention news, an SWE information packet, and subscription information for *U.S. Woman Engineer,* a magazine you'll find invaluable for the latest findings.

Send a self-addressed, stamped envelope to SWE at its headquarters at the United Engineering Center, Room 305, 345 East 47th Street, New York, New York 10017. Ask for "FACTS: An

Introduction to the Society of Women Engineers.'' Returning the coupon found in FACTS will get you on the mailing list for additional information. Bulletins and application forms describing the 38 scholarships SWE administers are also available; send a self-addressed, stamped envelope along with your request.

Deadline dates are extremely important. Applicants for freshman and reentry scholarships can receive applications from March through June. Those who apply for sophomore, junior, and senior scholarships can get applications only from October through January.

FINANCIAL AID FOR WOMEN AND MINORITIES

The good news is that financial aid is readily available for qualified women and minority students who want to pursue careers in technology, science, and engineering. Don't expect a full scholarship, however. You're more apt to be offered a ''package'' consisting of a partial scholarship, loans, and a part-time job. Internships and cooperative programs are excellent ways of helping to finance your college education.

You'll find *The Financial Aid Guide for Minority Engineering Scholars in Search of Scholarships, Grants and Loans* especially helpful. For a copy, write to National Action Council for Minorities in Engineering, Inc., 3 West 35th Street, New York, New York 10001.

National Achievement Scholarship Program for Outstanding Negro Students

This program, begun in 1964, was created specifically to provide recognition for able black youth and to increase their opportunities for higher education. The program honors academically promising high school students who are African Americans, and encourages them to continue their formal education. It also provides Achievement Scholarships for a substantial number of the most outstanding participants in the annual competition. Although Achievement Scholars report a wide variety of career plans, about 40 percent pursue college majors in engineering, mathematics, or science.

Between 1965 and 1990, more than 1.5 million black students from all parts of the country entered the Achievement Program. Some 106,000 of these students were honored and referred to U.S. colleges and universities in an effort to broaden their admission and financial aid opportunities. Within that time frame, Achievement Scholarships worth $43 million have been awarded to approximately 14,000 of the most outstanding program participants, and more than 2,800 of these young men and women currently are undergraduates at 275 of the nation's higher education programs.

Ninety percent of all Achievement Scholarships awarded in the first 26 competitions have been underwritten by independent sponsor organizations and a large number of program donors.

Each year, some 90,000 black students in more than 9,000 U.S. high schools compete for recognition and scholarships. To enter, students take the Preliminary Scholastic Aptitude Test/National Merit Scholarship Qualifying Test (PSAT/NMSQT)—usually in their junior year of high school. They mark a space on the test's answer sheet, identifying themselves as African Americans who want to be considered in this competition.

There are other criteria for eligibility; see your high school guidance counselor early in your junior year of high school (or even before) for details, or write to the National Achievement Scholarship Program for Outstanding Negro Students, One Rotary Center, 1560 Sherman Avenue, Evanston, Illinois 60201 for information.

Other Scholarships

Additional information on financial aid is available from the following organizations:

Bertha Lamme/Westinghouse Scholarships
 Society of Women Engineers
 United Engineering Center, Room 305
 345 East 47th Street
 New York, NY 10017

County 4-H Electric Awards Program
 National 4-H
 7100 Connecticut Avenue
 Chevy Chase, MD 20815

Engineering Program for the National Hispanic University
 255 East 14th Street
 Oakland, CA 94606

Financial Study Grant by the Society of Hispanic Professional Engineers
 P.O. Box 48 – Main Post Office
 Los Angeles, CA 90053

Incentive Grants Program, National Action Council for Minorities in Engineering (NACME)
 3 West 35th Street
 New York, NY 10001

Latin American Educational Foundation (LAEF)
 Suite 825
 303 West Colfax
 Denver, CO 80204

League of United Latin American Citizens (LULAC)
 P.O. Box 5135
 Corpus Christi, TX 78405

Leopold Schepp Foundation
 Suite 1900
 15 East 26th Street
 New York, NY 10010-1505

National Fund for Minority Engineering Students
1420 King Street
Alexandria, VA 22314

National Hispanic Scholarship Fund
Room 203 A
1400 Grant Avenue
Novato, CA 94947

Picket & Hatcher Educational Fund
P.O. Box 8169
Columbus, GA 31908

Science Talent Search Awards
Science Clubs of America
1719 N Street, NW
Washington, DC 20036

United States Senate Youth Program
William Randolph Hearst Fund–Suite 502
690 Market Street
San Francisco, CA 94104

MINORITY RECRUITMENT

Many engineering schools and companies recruit hard for qualified students. "Resumes from the campuses come to me after candidates have been prescreened by our recruiters," explains Lisa Chan, Chevron Chemical Company's human resources representative for professional recruiting. "I do further screening and send the resumes out to field sites for further candidate interviews. When I see resumes from females or under-represented minorities, especially from candidates whom our on-campus recruiters rate highly, I make a point of including them."

Sometimes the recruitment even starts before high school. Since 1983, more than two million seventh- and eighth-graders have taken part in MATHCOUNTS, a nationwide mathematics coaching and competition program aimed at combating math illiteracy in our nation's schools. For information, contact the National Society of Professional Engineers, (NPSE) Information Center, 1420 King Street, Alexandria, Virginia 22314.

In Pittsburgh, the Westinghouse High School of Science and Mathematics, open to all students, includes laboratory-centered instruction that emphasizes scientific process skills, funding for independent student research projects, one-on-one monitoring of student research activities by professional scientists and engineers, annual summer science camp and enrichment activities at Carnegie-Mellon University, and guaranteed scholarship assistance for all students completing the high school program.

Most engineering colleges and universities have special programs for culturally disadvantaged students. Minority students often take advantage of these programs. Notable is Georgia Tech's freshman engineering workshop, which invites ninth-grade students from minority backgrounds to visit the campus daily, meet with faculty, visit companies that employ engineers, and plan careers in engineering or related fields. More information on this program is available from the Director of Special Programs, College of Engineering, Georgia Institute of Technology, Atlanta, Georgia 30332.

Similar enrichment, awareness, or recruitment programs often exist at universities in metropolitan areas. Illinois Institute of Technology, for example, offers summer programs for talented, minority, Chicago-area high school juniors interested in math, science, or engineering; some scholarships are available. Write to the Illinois Institute of Technology, Engineering Department, 3300 South Federal, Chicago, Illinois 60616.

Also contact the University of Texas at Austin for information on its Equal Opportunities in Engineering Program, which includes scholarships. Write to the University of Texas–Austin,

Equal Opportunities in Engineering, College of Engineering, ECJ2-102, Austin, Texas 78712.

To locate such programs, ask your school guidance counselor for details or write to an affirmative action officer at a college or university near you.

Math and science are two important tools you'll need to qualify for well-paying jobs in plastics technology. Polymer chemistry, chemical engineering "process" courses, and materials-science courses in the properties of polymers are demanding, "hard" sciences. Finding opportunities for additional study and taking advantage of them may give you the edge you need for admission to a top-quality college or university program.

SPECIAL HELP

A number of organizations provide help, guidance, materials, and even scholarships to women and minority students who want to become engineers. While they aren't necessarily focused on plastics and plastics technology, nevertheless they're worth looking into.

Films about engineering your teacher can order directly and show in class include:

Bridging New Worlds (Uniendo Nuevos Mundos), a film in English with Spanish subtitles, to help parents and encourage their children to study engineering and the applied sciences. For information, contact: Bilingual Cine Television, 2601 Mission Street, Suite 703, San Francisco, California 94110.

Technology Occupations (order #VT-02), is a videotape for junior and senior high students that highlights careers in drafting, plastics, computer sciences, electrical technology, programming, and tool building. *Engineering Disciplines* (order #VT-01), also for junior and senior high students, highlights careers in structural, electrical, manufacturing, aeronautical, mechanical, and chemical engineering. Information on getting these videos is available from JETS, the Junior Engineering Technical Society, 1420 King Street, Suite 405, Alexandria, Virginia 22314-2715. JETS also has career literature available.

Ask JETS about the National Engineering Aptitude Search (NEAS). While it's not specifically aimed at women and minorities, the exam—a guidance-oriented test for high school students who are considering careers in engineering, math, science, or technology—helps determine students' strengths and weaknesses.

SOUTHEASTERN CONSORTIUM FOR MINORITIES

An organization that works closely with minority students is the Southeastern Consortium for Minorities in Engineering (SECME), currently involved with 256 high schools and approximately 20,000 students. For nearly 20 years, SECME has helped increase the number of minorities studying—and ultimately earning degrees in—engineering, mathematics, and science. SECME wants more "blue chip" graduates, defined by the organization as "marketable when they leave college, and more effective when they reach business and industry." SECME students compete for industry and university scholarships.

SECME programs, which include early intervention, concentrate on working with middle grade teachers to help them meet the needs of minority students and keep those students interested in math and science by "doing." SECME's cross-cultural workshops show teachers how to understand and value the cultural differences in the classroom, making teachers sensitive to students' needs, customs, traditions, and learning styles. Teachers learn how to help students work effectively as a team with classmates from different cultural backgrounds.

SECME's Summer Institute includes an annual student competition among high school finalists from the local and state levels. For information, write to the Southeastern Consortium for Minorities in Engineering (SECME), Georgia Institute of Technology, Atlanta, Georgia 30332-0270.

NATIONAL SOCIETY OF BLACK ENGINEERS

Another organization you'll find helpful is the National Society of Black Engineers (NSBE). Through national and regional conferences, NSBE encourages and advises disadvantaged youth to pursue engineering careers. A career fair, resume books, and technical seminars are part of the annual national conference.

Members of this student-run nonprofit organization visit schools and host junior and high school students on campuses. NSBE presents scholarships to high school seniors and, with support from the corporate sector, NSBE presents scholarships based on scholastic achievement.

For information, write to the National Society of Black Engineers (NSBE), 344 Commerce Street, Alexandria, Virginia 22314.

OTHER ORGANIZATIONS

If you are a minority student, especially if you're studying engineering, you'll want to take advantage of all the help that's available. Usually this includes summer programs before the freshman year of college; developmental year programs, which have special courses; and tutoring. Aggressively seek out such programs on your campus; taking part in them is well worth the time spent. If there are student chapters of national associations on your campus or senior chapters nearby, join, and attend meetings.

Here are several additional organizations that specifically target minorities, offering career information:

Hispanic Society of Engineers and Scientists (HSES)
P.O. Box 1393
Richland, WA 99352

Mexican-American Engineering Society (MAES)
P.O. Box 3520
Fullerton, CA 92634

Mid-America Consortium for Scientific and Engineering Achievement
c/o Engineering Department
Durland Hall, Kansas State University
Manhattan, KS 66506

*National Organization for Black Chemists and Chemical Engineers
c/o Howard University
Chemistry Department, 525 College Street
P.O. Box 5
Washington, DC 20059

National Action Council for Minorities in Engineering (NACME)
3 West 35th Street
New York, NY 10001

National Council of La Raza (NCLR)
955 L'Enfant Plaza SW, Suite 4000
Washington, DC 20024

Society for the Advancement of Chicanos and Native Americans in Science (SACNAS)
P.O. Box 30030
Bethesda, MD 20814

Society of Spanish Engineers, Planners & Architects
P.O. Box 75
Church Street Station
New York, NY 10007

ON THE JOB

If you've successfully completed your schooling, especially if you have an engineering degree, finding a job in the plastics industry and advancing your career should be fairly easy. In fact, college placement officers and executive search firms say you will be in demand. "There's no such thing as racial or sexual discrimination in this field," says Monroe Miller of Ryman, Bell, Green and Michaels, a Houston, Texas executive search firm.

Du Pont notes that during the years from 1984–1989, women have accounted for 33 percent and minorities 15 percent of the college graduates recruited by Du Pont in the United States. In 1989, 37 percent of college recruits were women, and 17 percent were minorities; more than 29 percent of the U.S. manager and other professionals promoted were women and/or minorities. At the end of 1989, 22 percent of the company's 28,000 U.S. managers and professional employees were women and/or minorities, a 38 percent increase over 1985.

The Bureau of Labor Statistics predicts a more culturally diverse work force in the next decade, with increased participation from women and minorities. For instance, BLS believes that within the work force, by the year 2000, the group with the largest numerical growth will be women in the prime working years, ages 25 to 54. This group is projected to increase by ten million, compared with the seven million increase in prime age men. In fact, says BLS, "prime age women not only would account for the largest labor force increase, but would also have the highest rate of growth."

Blacks in the labor force are expected to make up 12 percent of workers, up one percentage point from 1988—reflecting a higher growth rate than BLS projects for the overall labor force. The *participation rate* of Asians in the work force is projected to remain virtually the same as in 1990, but the numbers of Asians are growing at a rate of 3.6 percent annually—higher than either the black or white rate of increase, but below the rate increase projected for Hispanics. Between 1990 and 2000, says BLS, there will be an increase of 5.3 million Hispanics in the labor force—to 14.3 million in 2000, and Hispanics are projected to constitute 10 percent of the labor force, up three percentage points from 1988.

What do these figures mean for opportunities in plastics careers? More and more companies are beginning to realize that cultural diversity in the workplace not only is coming, but may, in fact, be helped along. Monsanto Chemical Company, for instance, points out that slightly over 50 percent of its new hires in 1989 were minority and women professionals; just under 40 percent of promotions in the same year also went to minority and women professionals.

Monsanto Chemical Company also offers employee seminars entitled "Managing a Diverse Work Force." Through these two-day seminars, by 1989, more than 2,500 employees became more sensitive to issues of race, sex, age, and culture.

As a supplement to these seminars, the chemical company conducts 14-day, intensive workshops on the ebb and flow of relationships. Graduates become inside consultants, available to anyone having a problem with a co-worker, subordinate, or boss.

For any given problem, two consultants are paired together as a team or, as Monsanto calls them, a "consulting pair." Often, these pairs reflect the racial or gender makeup of the individuals involved with the problem.

To get work relationships off to a good start, new employees go through a joining-up process in which they, their supervisor, and a pair of facilitators from the consulting-pairs program meet and talk. They deal immediately with biases that otherwise may not surface for months, if at all. Monsanto feels its program is effective and plans to continue the process.

While other plastics companies may not have the formal program Monsanto uses, if you're a woman or a member of a minority group, once you're working, you're part of a team. What counts then isn't *who* you are; it's what you know, what you're willing to learn, and how you perform.

CHAPTER 14

INTERNATIONAL OPPORTUNITIES

PLASTICS IN CANADA

While the Canadian plastics industry extends from coast to coast, most of its members are situated in Ontario, Quebec, British Columbia, and Alberta. The leading trade association, Society of the Plastics Industry (SPI) Canada, maintains a strong presence in those areas, with its head office in Toronto and regional offices in Montreal and Vancouver.

SPI Canada reports 1989 shipments by processors were $12.3 billion, up 3.4 percent over 1988, with shipments by the supplier groups (resins, machinery, and molds) at $4.4 billion, up 2.5 percent from 1988. A trade deficit estimated at over $1.2 billion exists, however—evenly divided between the United States at 49.3 percent and the rest of the world at 50.7 percent. However, *Canadian Chemical News* estimates that plastics processing is the largest secondary industry in British Columbia, providing the province with over 5,000 jobs. They also say that almost half of the sales processed in British Columbia were to markets outside of Canada.

One of the major educational programs in Canada is the British Columbia Institute of Technology's two-year plastics technology program. It graduates people qualified to work at the senior machine-operation level, as well as in research and development, technical service, machine setting, product design, inspection, and quality control.

Additional Jobs

Plastics processors continued to add more jobs in 1989. Employment by Canadian processors reached 106,700—up 8.1 percent from 1988. New investment in plant, machinery, and equipment in the plastics processing industry in 1989 increased 6.7 percent over 1988.

In 1989, a major study, "Report on Human Resource Planning for the Canadian Plastics Processing Industry," recommended support for industry efforts to establish a Canadian plastics training center. The center would act as the appropriate industry-driven facility to deliver short-duration training programs aimed at upgrading industry skill levels.

Automotive: Fastest Growing Market

A study titled "Canadian Plastics End-Use Markets Analysis 1986–1996," published jointly by Industry, Science & Technology Canada and SPI Canada, identifies the automotive industry as the fastest growing market for the Canadian plastics industry. Projected growth rates for plastic consumption in Canadian-produced vehicles are 8.7 percent in 1986 to 1991 and somewhat over 9 percent in 1991 to 1996.

One of the leading trade publications covering developments in plastics markets and technology is *Canadian Plastics*. Its ten issues a year cover major highlights, and its November/December issue publishes a "plastics calendar," listing all important dates for seminars, trade shows, and conferences in the coming year.

Schools and Training

For information about plastics education in Canada, write the following:

Ahuntsic College
 155 St. Hubert Street
 Montreal, Quebec, Canada H2M 1Y8

Berkeley College
 155 St. Hubert Street
 Montreal, Quebec, Canada H2M 1Y8

British Columbia Institute of Technology
 3700 Willingdon Avenue
 Burnaby, British Columbia, Canada V5G 3H2

College de la region de l'amiante
 671 Boulevard Smith Sud
 Thetford Mines, Quebec, Canada G6G 1N1

Ecole Polytechnique
 P.O. Box 6079, Station "A"
 Montreal, Quebec, Canada H3C 3A7

McMaster University
 Department of Chemical Engineering
 Hamilton, Ontario, Canada L0H 4M6

Northern Alberta Institute of Technology
 Department of Advanced Education & Manpower
 11762–106 Street
 Edmonton, Alberta, Canada T5G 2R1

Ryerson Polytechnical Institute
 50 Gould Street
 Toronto, Ontario, Canada M5B 1E8

Write to National Commission for Cooperative Education, 360 Huntington Avenue, Boston, Massachusetts 02115, U.S.A., for

Undergraduate Programs of Cooperative Education in the United States and Canada.

Write to CED Directory, P.O. Box M, Mississippi State, Mississippi 39762, U.S.A., for *Engineering Co-Op Directory,* a complete directory of all co-op engineering in the United States and Canada.

Canadian Organizations

The following organizations have information and material on the Canadian plastics industry:

Association of Canadian Industrial Designers
 c/o Humber College
 205 Humber College Boulevard
 Etobicoke, Ontario, Canada M9W 5L7

Association of Consulting Engineers of Canada
 130 Albert Street, Suite 616
 Ottawa, Ontario, Canada K1P 5G4

Association des designers industriels du Quebec
 407 Saint-Laurent Boulevard, Suite 500
 Montreal, Quebec, Canada H2Y 2Y5

Automotive Parts Manufacturers' Association of Canada
 1 University Avenue, Suite 602
 P.O. Box 43
 Toronto, Ontario, Canada M5J 2P1

The Canadian Chemical Producers' Association
 350 Sparks Street, Suite 805
 Ottawa, Ontario, Canada K1R 7S8

The Canadian Manufacturers' Association
 1 Yonge Street, 14th floor
 Toronto, Ontario, Canada M5E 1J9

Canadian Plastics Institute
 1262 Don Mills Road, Suite 48
 Don Mills, Ontario, Canada M3B 2W7

Canadian Society for Chemical Engineering
  1785 Alta Vista Drive, Suite 300
  Ottawa, Ontario, Canada K1G 3Y6

Canadian Society for Chemistry
  1785 Alta Vista Drive, Suite 300
  Ottawa, Ontario, Canada K1G 3Y6

Canadian Standards Association
  178 Rexdale Boulevard
  Rexdale, Ontario, Canada M9W 1R3

Canadian Urethane Manufacturers' Association
  32 Baleberry Crescent
  Weston, Ontario, Canada M9P 3L2

Chemical Institute of Canada
  1785 Alta Vista Drive, Suite 300
  Ottawa, Ontario, Canada K1G 3Y6

Packaging Association of Canada
  111 Merton Street, Suite 201
  Toronto, Ontario, Canada M4S 3A7

Quebec Plastics and Rubber Group
  8710 Pascal-Gaignon Street
  St. Leonard, Quebec, Canada H1P 1Y8

The Rubber Association of Canada
  89 Queensway West, Suite 308
  Mississauga, Ontario, Canada L5B 2V2

Sign Association of Canada
  7030 Woodbine Avenue, Unit 500
  Markham, Ontario, Canada L3O 1A3

Societe de developpement industriel du Quebec
  Mercantile Place
  770 Sherbrooke Street East, 9th floor
  Montreal, Quebec, Canada H3H 1G1

Society of Packaging and Handling Engineers
  95 Orfus Road
  Toronto, Ontario, Canada M6A 1M4

Society of the Plastics Industry of Canada
   1262 Don Mills Road
   Don Mills, Ontario, Canada M3B 2W7

Vinyl Council of Canada
   1262 Don Mills Road, Suite 104
   Don Mills, Ontario, Canada M3B 2W7

Windsor Alliance of Moldmakers
   749 Walker Road
   Windsor, Ontario, Canada N8Y 2N2

OPPORTUNITIES IN GREAT BRITAIN

One of the main sources of information about the plastics industry in Britain and the United Kingdom is the British Plastics Federation, 5 Belgrave Square, London SW1X 8PH. Also helpful, and found at the same London address, is the Plastics and Rubber Advisory Service—part of the British Plastics Federation.

You can also obtain information from the Plastic and Rubber Institute, 11 Hobart Place, London SW1 OHL. Two other good sources are the Polymer Education & Training Information Service, 5 Belgrave Square, London SW1X OHL and Plastics Processing Industry Training Board (PPITB), Coppice House, Halesford 7, Teleford, Shropshire TF7 4NA.

Recommended Publications

The following publications are especially recommended. Reading them will help you keep up with trade news and developments.

Plastics & Rubber Weekly
   P.O. Box 109
   19 Scarbrook Road
   Croydon CR4 1QH

British Plastics & Rubber
  9 Weir Road
  London SW12 OLT

Plastics & Rubber International
  2nd floor, 2 Park Lane
  Croydon CRO 1JA

International Reinforced Plastics
  Loudwater House
  High Wycobe HP10 9TL

Advanced Composites Engineering
  The Design Council
  28 Haymarket
  London Surrey GU2 5BH

Plastics & Rubber Today
  P.O. Box 109
  19 Scarbrook Road
  Croydon CR4 1QH

European Plastics News
  Quadrant House
  Sutton
  Surrey SM2 5AS

Reinforced Plastics
  Mayfield House
  256 Banbury Road
  Oxford OX2 7DH

High Performance Plastics
  Mayfield House
  256 Banbury Road
  Oxford OX2 7DH

Composites
  P.O. Box 63—Westbury House
  Bury Street
  Guildford SW1Y 4SU

Leading schools offering courses in polymers, rubbers, and related subjects include:

Polytechnic of North London
   London School of Polymer Technology, Polytechnical
   North London, Holloway Road
   London N7 8BD

Plastics Processing Industry Training Centre
   Course Administration Service
   Halesfield 7
   Tetford TF7 4QL

Queens University, Belfast
   Mechanical and Manufacturing Engineering Department
   Queens University, Ashby Building
   Stranmills Road
   Belfast, Northern Ireland BT9 5AH

Lancaster University
   Chemistry Department
   Lancaster University, Bailrigg
   Lancaster Lancs LA1 4YA

Manchester Polytechnic
   School of Polymer Technology/Chemistry Department
   Faculty of Science & Engineering
   Chester Street
   Manchester
   Greater Manchester M1 5GD

U.M.L.S.T.
   Materials Science Centre
   UMIST, Grosvenor Street
   Manchester, Greater Manchester M1 7HS

Burton upon Trent Technical College
   Lichfield Street
   Burton upon Trent
   Staffordshire DE14 3RL

London School of Polymer Technology
   Poly of North London
   Holloway Road
   London N7 8DB

Trowbridge Technical College
Centre for Polymer Studies
College Road, Trowbridge
Wiltshire BA14 OES

OPPORTUNITIES IN AUSTRALIA

One of the most useful sources for information about plastics (which are polymers) is a report from the Department of Industry, Technology and Commerce on polymer technology in Australia. Written by F. M. Karpfen of the Strategic Industrial Research Branch and Dr. S. Nagarajan of the Resource-based Industries Branch, the report describes Australian industries that produce and process polymers and products that contain polymers. It was prepared in the New Materials Technology Section, Engineering Branch, Heavy Industries Division, and was published by the Australian Government Publishing Service.

Australian polymer producers generally fall into two groups. Some are wholly-owned subsidiaries of multinational companies; others have principal shareholders which are multinational companies. The producers are located in New South Wales, Victoria, and Queensland. Other companies (known as compounders) convert the resins into material for plastics processors to use.

In contrast to the resin producers, the majority of companies that process or fabricate plastics in Australia are relatively small, with only a few large firms. About eight out of ten of these companies are Australian-owned. Figures from the Australian Bureau of Statistics show that in 1984–1985, over half of these companies had under ten employees.

Just under 40 percent of plastics processing companies were located in New South Wales; a similar percentage were located in Victoria. Others are found in Queensland and South Australia.

140   Opportunities in Plastics Careers

More than one-fifth of polymers Australia consumes are used in packaging. Others are used in composites, adhesives and sealants, and paints. Most Australian-made plastics are consumed within the country; actually, Australia imports about 15 percent of the plastic products it uses.

The plastics products manufacturing sector is one of the fastest-growing sectors of the Australian manufacturing industry, since its diverse products are used in virtually all other industries. In 1987–1988, the value of production in major plastic product manufacturing sectors included $1,262 million (Australian dollars) for flexible packaging and abrasive papers, $146 million (Australian dollars) for rigid plastic sheeting and floor coverings, and $2,992 million (Australian dollars) for other plastic products.

One Industry Profile, produced in 1990 for Australia's Business Migration Program, says important growth areas include the development of high performance polymers and advanced composites. Now polymers are being developed for structural applications in the automotive industry, with plastic use expected to increase by approximately 100 kilograms per passenger motor vehicle. Significant investments have been made in new or replacement equipment and machinery. In June 1988, plastic product manufacturing establishments with four or more persons employed a total of 36,430 persons.

Organizations

The Plastics Institute of Australia (PIA) is the umbrella organization for 15 groups involved with polymer technologies. PIA is recognized as the trade association for the plastics industry. It publishes a journal (*Plastics News*); organizes exhibitions, seminars, and conferences; and has helped to set up training centers for plastics skills.

Also active is the Plastics and Rubber Institute (Australian Section), whose members are primarily technologists who work in the plastics and rubber industries. The Polymer Division of the Royal Australian Chemical Institute, whose members are individuals, not companies, organizes national meetings on polymers every 15–18 months, runs short courses and workshops, and publishes a newsletter and directory.

You may also wish to contact the Plastics Industry Association of Australia at 41–43 Exhibition Street, Melbourne, Victoria 3000.

Schools and Universities

The following addresses may prove useful for obtaining additional information:

Chisholm Institute of Technology
P.O. Box 197
Caulfield East
Victoria 3145

Griffith University
Natham
Brisbane
Queensland 4111

Macquarie University
North Ryde
New South Wales 2113

Monash University
Clayton
Victoria 3168

University of Technology/Sydney
Broadway
Sydney
New South Wales 2007

James Cook University of North Queensland
  Townsville
  Queensland 4811

Queensland Institute of Technology
  Brisbane
  Queensland 4000

Royal Melbourne Institute of Technology
  Box 2476V GPO
  Melbourne
  Victoria 3001

Swinburne Institute of Technology
  P.O. Box 218
  Hawthorn
  Victoria 3122

University of Melbourne
  Victoria 3052

University of Queensland
  Brisbane
  Queensland 4067

University of Adelaide
  Box 498 GPO
  Adelaide
  South Australia 5001

University of Sydney
  New South Wales 2006

  It may also prove useful to contact the New Materials Technology Section, Engineering Branch, Heavy Industries Division, Canberra National Convention Centre, Canberra City, ACT 2601, Australia, for additional information.

APPENDIX A
PERIODICALS

Plastics technology is described in a number of journals and trade publications. Many—not all—of them are cited in *Applied Science and Technology Index,* a reference set usually available at your public library or college information center. Others are tracked through *Business Periodicals Index,* a similar publication also found at libraries. You'll use *Applied Science and Technology Index* to keep up with technical and engineering developments in plastics technology. You'll find *Business Periodicals Index* most useful in learning about the financial side of the plastics industry: sales and marketing trends, company-by-company information, and mergers and acquisitions.

The easiest way to use a reference set such as *Applied Science and Technology Index* is to start with the most recent bound volume—that is, a full year's worth of articles. Under the general heading "Plastics," you'll find "see also . . ." followed by a long list of subtopics such as "molds (for plastics)," "methacrylates," "polystyrene," and "thermosets." It's a good idea to photocopy the list of "see also" headings, so you don't have to keep referring back to the general heading. You can also photocopy the lists of articles cited under the particular subtopics that interest you.

The paper-bound supplements that are issued during the year will have more recent articles, but of course not every subtopic will be covered. Starting your research with the most recent bound volume gives you a more complete list of subtopics and a better idea of what's available.

Your reference librarian will help you locate articles in the periodicals your library carries and can often suggest where to get the publications it doesn't. If you live near a major city or industrial region, company libraries at research centers, manufacturing plants, or corporate offices often subscribe to specialized journals. Usually such libraries have agreements with your local library so patrons of the public library can make special arrangements to use the company libraries.

The following periodicals are especially useful to those interested in a career in plastics technology. If your library doesn't have them, or you're not sure if you want to subscribe, write to the Managing Editor of the publication. Ask for subscription information, enclose a check, and request a sample issue. You can find the price per issue by checking *Gale Directory of Publications and Broadcast Media* (formerly *Ayer's*), available at your library's reference desk.

Periodicals

Chemical Engineering
 1221 Avenue of the Americas
 New York, NY 10020

Chemical & Engineering News
 1155 16th Street, NW
 Washington, DC 20036

Chemical Week
 1221 Avenue of the Americas
 New York, NY 10020

Material Engineering
 1100 Superior Avenue
 Cleveland, OH 44114

Modern Plastics
 1221 Avenue of the Americas
 New York, NY 10020

Packaging Digest
 122 East 42nd Street
 New York, NY 10168

Plastics Compounding
 1129 East 17th Avenue
 Denver, CO 80218

Plastics Connection
 PO Box 814
 Amherst, MA 01004

Plastics Design Forum
 1129 East 17th Avenue
 Denver, CO 80218

Plastics Design & Processing
 17730 Peterson Road
 Libertyville, IL 60048

Plastics Engineering
 14 Fairfield Drive
 Brookfield Center, CT 06805

Plastics Industry News
 1129 East 17th Avenue
 Denver, CO 80218

Plastics Machinery & Equipment
 1129 East 17th Avenue
 Denver, CO 80218

Plastics Packaging
 1129 East 17th Avenue
 Denver, CO 80218

Plastics Technology
633 Third Avenue
New York, NY 10017

Plastics World
275 Washington Street
Newton, MA 02158

Information for Women and Minorities

The following publications will be of special interest to you if you're a woman or member of a minority group interested in an engineering career:

Career Guide for Minority Students Interested in Engineering
School of Engineering and Applied Science
George Washington University
Washington, DC 20052

Minorities in Engineering: A Blueprint for Action
Alfred P. Sloan Foundation
30 Fifth Avenue
New York, NY 10020

The Woman Engineer Magazine
Equal Opportunity Publications
411 Broadway
Greenlawn, NY 11740

Hispanic Engineer
280 South Sadler Avenue
Los Angeles, CA 90022

The Minority Engineer Magazine
Equal Opportunity Publications
44 Broadway
Greenlawn, NY 11740

Check the "videos" section of this chapter for other resources for women and minorities.

Reports, Technical Papers, Directories

ANTEC 88: Plastics Are Shaping Tomorrow Today. Pasadena, California: Techtonic, 1988. (Society of Plastics Engineers Annual Technical Conference Proceedings, 46th)

Corneliussen, Roger D., ed. *Drexel Polymer Notes (DPN).* Philadelphia, Pennsylvania. (Monthly journal that comprehensively surveys research developments in the field of polymer materials)

Drozda, T.J., ed. *Composite Applications: The Future Is Now.* Dearborn, Michigan: Society of Manufacturing Engineers, 1989. (31 technical papers)

Plastics Institute of America, Inc. *Foodplas VII-'90.* Hoboken, New Jersey, 1990. (Conference Proceedings)

Plastics Institute of America, Inc. *Recyclingplas II Conference Proceedings.* Hoboken, New Jersey, 1990.

The Gary Siegel Organization, Inc. *Issues and Trends in the Plastics and Rubber Industries, an Industry Study Prepared for Berger, Goldstein Capital Group, Inc.* Chicago, Illinois, June 1990.

Society of Manufacturing Engineers, *Directory of Composites Manufacturers, Suppliers, Consultants and Research Organizations.* Dearborn, Michigan, 1990.

Society of Manufacturing Engineers, *Directory of Manufacturing Education in Colleges, Universities, and Technical Institutes.* Dearborn, Michigan, 1990.

Society of Plastics Engineers Staff, *ANTEC '86: Plastics—Value Through Technology: 44th Annual Technical Conference & Exhibit, 1986.* Ann Arbor, Michigan: Books on Demand, University of Michigan Institute.

Society of Plastics Engineers, *Listing of Institutions which Offer Graduate or Undergraduate Plastics/Polymer Programs in the United States and Canada,* Brookfield, Connecticut, annual.

Plastics Institute of America, Inc., staff edited, *Plastics Recycling as a Future Business Opportunity.* Lancaster, Pennsylvania; Technomics, 1988. (Collection of papers from Recyclingplas III conference)

Society of the Plastics Industry, Inc. *Facts & Figures of the U.S. Plastics Industry.* Washington, D.C., annual.

Society of the Plastics Industry, Inc. *Labor Survey, Plastics Processing Companies.* Washington, D.C., annual. (Also available: *Financial and Operating Ratios Survey, Salary and Sales Policy Survey,* and *Employee Benefits Survey*)

U.S. Congress, Office of Technology Assessment, *Advanced Materials by Design: New Structural Materials Technologies,* OTA E-351. Washington, D.C.: U. S. Government Printing Office, June 1988.

U.S. Congress, Office of Technology Assessment, *Facing America's Trash: What Next for Municipal Solid Waste?* OTA-O-424. Washington, D.C.: U.S. Government Printing Office, October 1989.

U.S. Congress, Office of Technology Assessment, *Making Things Better: Competing in Manufacturing,* OTA-ITE-443. Washington, D.C.: U.S. Government Printing Office, February 1990.

U.S. Department of Labor, Bureau of Labor Statistics, *Employment and Earnings.* Washington, D.C., August 1990.

U.S. Department of Labor, Bureau of Labor Statistics, *Outlook 2000.* Washington, D.C. April 1990.